The Indoor Gardener's

How-to-Build-It Book

JACK KRAMER

Drawings by Adrián Martínez and James Carew

SIMON AND SCHUSTER · NEW YORK

Designed by Eve Metz
Manufactured in the United States of America

1 2 3 4 5 6 7 8 9 10

Library of Congress Cataloging in Publication Data:
Kramer, Jack, 1927–
    The indoor gardener's how-to-build-it book.

    1. Container gardening—Equipment and supplies.
2. Plastics craft. 3. House plants. I. Title.
SB418.K75   681′.7631   74–13528
ISBN 0–671–21843–3

Acknowledgments

The companies involved in the manufacture of acrylic plastics have been especially helpful to me, contributing brochures and photos and helpful information. I owe thanks to these organizations:

Rohm and Haas Co.
E. I. Du Pont de Nemours & Co., Inc.
American Cyanamid Co.

To my designer, Adrián Martínez, I am again grateful. He and I worked out the various designs you see in the drawings. A special vote of thanks goes to Andrew R. Addkison, A.I.D., head of the Environmental Design Department of the California College of Arts and Crafts, for his valuable suggestions in strengthening this book.

Jack Kramer

CONTENTS

CONTENTS

INTRODUCTION:
Plants in a New Dimension

Today, whether in apartment or house, most people who grow plants soon realize that there are many more ways to enjoy them than just for the satisfaction of seeing them grow. The pot on the windowsill is still with us, but plants in terrariums, in hanging containers and in other special displays increase their beauty and importance many times over as part of the design of the room.

Working with plants for the past fifteen years, I have discovered they often need suitable accessories to better display or grow them. But these items, such as pedestals and plant platforms and plant stands, are generally not available in great variety commercially (or if they are they are rarely attractive), and often they do not fit the particular place in a room where you want a plant. So I started making what I call my own "plant helpers" and I found acrylic sheets the easiest and best material to use. Acrylic is easy to work with and, with new adhesives, simple to put together. I discovered I could make almost any size container in almost any design; and the transparent quality of acrylic would always be highly decorative and uncluttered-looking in any room.

INTRODUCTION

You do not have to be a skilled craftsman—God knows, I never have been—to make these projects. Through the years I have custom designed and built many terrariums and plant stands, hanging containers and other time-saving items that are not available commercially, and it was only my interest in special plant needs that provided an incentive. That is what this book is all about—it is a compilation of handmade plant helpers you can make at home to help yourself and to help your plants. In all cases I have included step-by-step drawings to show you how to make these items, along with descriptive text to tell you how to use them for plants. In addition, at the back of the book you will find a comprehensive list of plants for the furniture you have made. With this book in hand, I hope you will be inspired to get your fingers going and your imagination in action to really enjoy your plants.

Jack Kramer

1·A Multitude of Uses

You finally buy that lovely dieffenbachia at the nursery, but when you get it into the living room it is too small, and hardly in scale with the rest of the room furnishings. You are disappointed—but you do not have to be, because on a handcrafted pedestal the plant will look just fine. No, you will not find an inexpensive commercial pedestal—few are made—but by using acrylic sheets you can make one to suit the space. When you make it yourself, the pedestal can be any height, any design *you want*. And you will find that working with acrylics is easier than you imagined.

Terrariums intrigue you, but the commercial containers are expensive, not suitable for the kind of small garden you want, or not esthetically pleasing. Or you may want a compartmented terrarium—something unique. Do not despair—you can handcraft this garden for tiny plants from acrylic and wood in a few hours and have the satisfaction of knowing you made it yourself.

Hanging baskets of plants are popular, and you think that some of them would provide vertical accent and color for that dining-room area. But how do you water them without having water stain the floors? Once again, with little effort and cost you can make a plastic container that will accommodate the plants and be as good as—and probably better than—any you could buy.

Such is the variety of things you can make from acrylics. But to make them you need to know something about the material you are working with. The text that follows describes acrylic— what it can or cannot do for you in designing your own custom furniture for your plants.

"Plastic" through the years has become a word that covers a multitude of products, and as such it has confused the average person. There are many plastics: for example, there is the corrugated rigid material used for fences or temporary roofing; there is the flexible plastic (almost like Saran Wrap) that has been used for temporary greenhouses or lath-house roofing; there is screening plastic—plastic with wire mesh; and there are, of course, plastic materials used for household articles such as shower curtains.

In this book we are concerned with thermoplastics—hard and rigid materials at normal temperatures but soft and·malleable when subjected to extremely high heat. In particular, we talk about acrylic, a man-made substance that contains natural or synthetic organic compounds. The technical nature of the product is not important to us here; what is important is that acrylics are tough, transparent materials that adapt to myriad uses. In recent years we have seen them used for book holders, shelving and furniture.

Acrylics are easy to work with and in simple designs have a definite appeal for the do-it-yourselfer. Unlike glass, acrylic does not readily break, so cutting yourself is not a hazard. It is lightweight, easy to lift and move about, and most important, perhaps, it can be cemented easily. And the cement, a fusion-type epoxy, bonds acrylic pieces together with great strength.

For use in the home, acrylic gives a clean, simple, but elegant look to finished pieces. And unlike plastics of years ago, the product does not yellow or discolor with time, although it does scratch if handled roughly. In room interiors acrylics lend an airy, light feeling—a definite plus in small apartments, where plant furniture must never appear cumbersome or heavy.

I found, as I worked on this book, that most people think acrylics are terribly expensive. This was true years ago, but

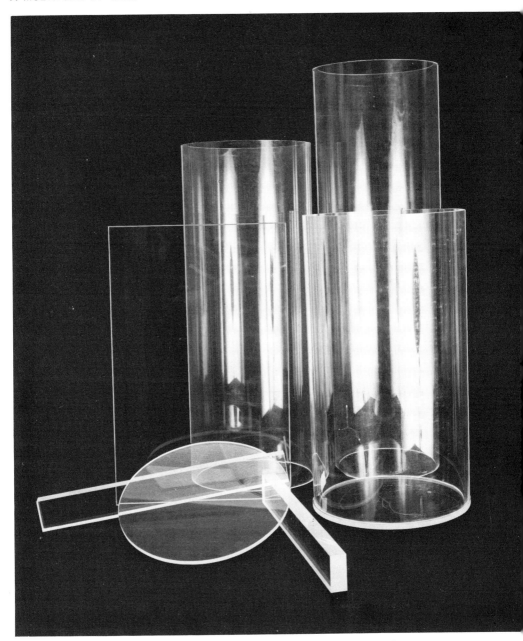

Acrylic comes in tubes, bars and flat sheets and can be sawed and cut to desired dimensions to make many different "plant helper" projects. (Photo by Clark Photo/Graphic)

not today. The cost of acrylic is moderate and well within the budget of the average person because improved production methods and the increased use of acrylics for furniture and other household items have brought the price down. For example, a 12 by 36-inch sheet of ¼-inch acrylic costs little more than regular glass of the same size. A cylinder (called a tube in the industry) 8 inches in diameter and 14 inches high is slightly higher in price but still not exorbitant. Colored acrylic is more expensive than clear. A mirrored finished acrylic, a recent product, is, at this writing, quite expensive, but it does have the added advantage of acting as a mirror.

Acrylics are now available from various dealers throughout the United States; a list of places to buy materials is at the end of this book.

Types, Sizes and Properties

Acrylic, the revolutionary new plastic material introduced in the 1930s, became an important product for many uses because of its light weight, strength, optical clarity, weather resistance and ability to be easily machined and shaped. Acrylic sheets are available in various thicknesses: ⅛-inch, 3/16-inch, ¼-inch; and sizes vary from 18 by 24 inches to large sheets. Tubes (cylinders), bars and rods are also sold in varying dimensions. When buying acrylics, always tell the dealer they are for decorative use, not for glazing projects.

Depending upon the manufacturer, acrylic sheets are called Plexiglas® (Rohm & Haas Co.), Acrylite (American Cyanamid Co.), or Lucite (E. I. Du Pont de Nemours & Co., Inc). Recently Rohm & Haas Co. introduced the Plexiglas mirror; this has a wide range of applications, and, like other acrylics, can be drilled and sawed, so it is very versatile. Another new product is Du Pont Co.'s Abcite, a coated acrylic sheet with scratch-resistant qualities.

No matter which brand you select, acrylic sheets transmit more than 90 percent of the light. Acrylic has a brilliant and crystal clarity and gives an illusion of depth because light striking it at certain angles is reflected back into the material. This light-

Tubes or cylinders can be used as plant pedestals by slipping potted plants in place; pot rim rests on edges. To catch excess water, clay saucers filled with gravel can be placed at bottom. In this manner evaporated water provides additional humidity for plant roots. (Photo by Clark Photo/Graphic)

diffusing characteristic is highly desirable: lighted plastic appears to glow.

Acrylic sheet is strong enough to take considerable abuse. It can be bent or twisted; it withstands shock and vibration. And it is less than half as heavy as glass sheets of the same size.

You can work acrylic sheet with ordinary saws, drills and other tools. To make various projects in this book you will need a vise, coping saw, handsaw or hacksaw, hand drill, crosscut hand files, flat-nose and round-nose pliers, and sandpaper.

One word of warning: acrylics are combustible materials, so observe fire precautions as you would if you were working with wood.

Plant Helpers

Let us take a quick look at the many things you can build for your plants with acrylic sheet, by itself or in combination with wood. These are just some of the items we have made (detailed in later chapters):

Plant pedestals
Plant platforms
Plant holders
Hanging terrariums
Plant stands
Window shelves
Wall shelves
Propagating cases
Small greenhouses
Artificial-light unit
Terrariums
Planters:
    Cubes
    Rectangles
    Triangles
    Cylinders

None of the above projects should take more than a few hours to build; none should be exorbitant in price; and all can be made to fit a specific need. Some can be used as furniture (pedestals, shelving); others are specifically for plants. And best of all, once you have made these simple units you will find you can also make tables and stands and sundry items for home use with little time and effort. Indeed, add a top to many of the planters and they can become end tables or other pieces of substantial furniture for your home.

So, if you are irritated by high prices in furniture, or by having to buy what is available and not what you want, take acrylic in hand, get tools ready, and get started!

Several Plexiglas plant helpers are shown here—a handsome window shelf, a hanging planter and the unique stepladder plant stand. (Photo courtesy Rohm and Haas Co.)

16

OTHER MATERIALS

Most of the plant furniture and plant helpers in this book are specifically designed for acrylic sheets. However, in many cases, wood or glass may be substituted as working materials with satisfactory results—for example, in the artificial-light unit in Chapter 6 and the stacking plant cubes in Chapter 3.

Indeed, many of the designs in the drawings are easily adaptable to these materials, so if you prefer wood or glass, use them. Wood, of course, will give a heavier feeling to a unit than acrylic, but sometimes a more stable feeling in plant furniture is desirable. Glass, like acrylic, has a light and airy look; its disadvantage is that it may break if dropped or incorrectly cut.

This attractive acrylic plant stand will suit almost any room decor. The plant may be placed within a cylinder in the planter or can be planted directly in the pedestal compartment. (Photo by Clark Photo/Graphic)

A group of acrylic cylinders can decorate a corner and still retain a light airy feeling. Use 8- or 10-inch cylinders of varying heights. The plants are plectranthus (left) and coleus. (Photo by Clark Photo/ Graphic)

2·Working with Acrylic Sheet

Acrylic is no more difficult to work with than wood, and in some cases it may be easier; for example, cutting and drilling holes are simple procedures. At the start, use some scrap pieces for practice, to gain confidence and to see how easy it is.

General Tips

Try, as a usual procedure, to buy acrylic cut to size rather than in large stock sheets, which are awkward to handle. The cost of cut-to-size material is not that much more than stock material, and working with small sheets is easier than working with large ones.

Always protect the surface of acrylic. The material has high luminosity and can be scratched easily (unless you are using Abcite), which is why the adhesive paper that acrylic is covered with should be left on as long as possible while you are working the material.

Do all your cutting, drilling and edge polishing before you remove the paper. Do not work on rough or dirty surfaces because sliding the material over them could cause scratching, even with the paper on.

Place sheets vertically, standing on edge, if you want to store them for any length of time. If they are laid at an angle and not fully supported, they can warp. If a sheet does warp, lay it flat for several days until it is straight again. Store the largest pieces on the bottom so they do not overhang smaller pieces and warp. Prolonged exposure to heat, sun or moisture will cause the adhesive on the protective paper to become hard, making it difficult to remove. If this happens, use alcohol to release the paper from the sheet. Keep materials in a cool, clean, dark place to avoid this problem.

Cutting

Thin sheets of acrylic (up to ³⁄₁₆-inch thick, 8 to 12 inches long) can be cut in the same manner as glass. Make a deep cut with a scriber or engravers' marker (available from suppliers), and use a steel ruler to guide the cut, holding it securely flat against the sheet. It is absolutely essential that pieces be cut squarely and precisely, or cementing will become a problem. Repeat the scribing cut several times; do not move the ruler or the cut will be jagged.

Cutting thin Plexiglas is easily done with a scribing tool or cutting tool (from dealers). Note that masking tape remains in place during this procedure. (Photo courtesy Rohm and Haas Co.)

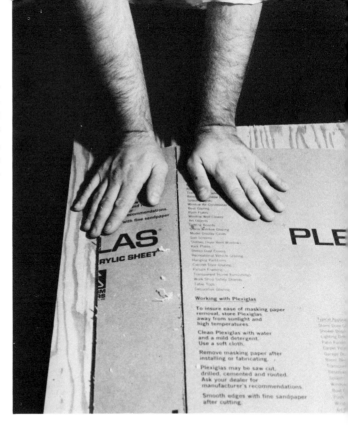

To break Plexiglas, apply equal pressure on each side of cut line. Use wood dowel under the length of the intended break. Minimum cutoff width is about 1½ inches. (Photo courtesy Rohm and Haas Co.)

Now lay the piece, scribe face up, on a wooden dowel, mop handle, or wooden pencil. Be sure the wooden support is as long as the cut. Hold the piece down with one hand; apply pressure with the other hand. Work your hands along the scribe line as the break progresses.

Sawing

Larger and thicker sheets of acrylic (³⁄₁₆-inch, ¼-inch, ⅜-inch) must be cut with a band, saber, electric hand, or circular table saw. You can easily make straight cuts once you acquire some experience, so do some practicing beforehand on scrap pieces, as previously mentioned, and remember that you *must* saw acrylic slowly and carefully. If you use a table saw, make certain the fence is firmly in place before you start to cut. *Never* use a wooden blade; you want a metal cutting blade that has approximately 15 teeth to the inch and is at least ⅜-inch wide. Feed sheets slowly into a blade, with one edge firmly pressed against

23

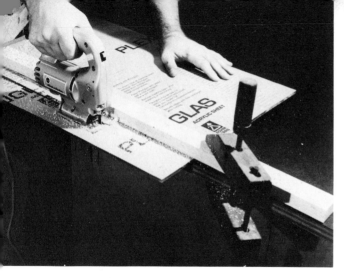

For heavy Plexiglas use a saber or band saw. Hold material down firmly when cutting and do not force it to the blade. (Photo courtesy Rohm and Haas Co.)

the fence, using a slight pressure. Then move the sheet steadily, but not fast. To decrease the chances of chipped edges, feed the sheet slowly both at the beginning and at the end of the process. To minimize vibration, which causes crazing (cracking) and chipping, be sure the sheet is firmly on the table. After a while the protective paper on the sheet will begin to stick to the blade, so coat the blade periodically with old candle wax or soap.

If you use a hand saw, first mark the pattern onto the sheet and then cut slowly and firmly to minimize vibration. The hand saw should have at least 6 teeth per inch. Always support the part of the sheet that extends beyond the table.

Use a saber or band saw to make curved and irregular cuts in acrylic. First trace the pattern onto masking paper; then carefully move the blade along the tracing. Once again, avoid vibration, which can cause chipping of the edges.

Here a circular saw is used to cut Plexiglas. (Photo courtesy Rohm and Haas Co.)

Sawed edges can be sanded smooth with medium grit (60–80) sandpaper. (Photo courtesy Rohm and Haas Co.)

Filing and Sanding

When you finish cutting acrylic there will be saw marks; eliminate them by filing or sanding. To file off saw marks, put the acrylic in a padded vise or clamp, and with a flat file (place the file's face parallel to the edge being worked) file at a slight angle in one direction until edges become shiny and brilliant. (Masking paper remains on acrylic while filing.) Use a wire brush to remove file chips from the blade.

To sand off file marks, use medium-grit (80 to 100) sandpaper. Place the sheet upright in padded clamps and wrap sandpaper around a sanding block (a piece of wood). Keep the face of the sanding block parallel to the plastic and rub vigorously until the saw marks are gone. Now use 180- to 220-grit sandpaper to polish the edges. Moisten the paper somewhat to prevent clogging and heat friction. Repeat the process, now using 280- to 320-grit sandpaper. You will note as you sand that the edges become shinier, more finished. A final sanding with 500- to 600-grit sandpaper is sometimes required to attain the mirrorlike finish on edges that signifies a finished piece.

To get a transparent edge on Plexiglas after sanding, use a muslin wheel with a good grade of fine-grit buffing compound. Remove masking tape when buffing edges. (Photo courtesy Rohm and Haas Co.)

Drilling

Drilling into acrylic is somewhat different from drilling into wood, so it is best to practice a few times before proceeding to the actual piece. You can use either an electric hand drill or manual drill to make holes in acrylic. The edges of ordinary metal-twist drill bits may crack the acrylic, so use special acrylic drill bits (available from suppliers). When drilling acrylic with power tools, work much slower than you would when drilling wood or metal. Clamp the sheet of acrylic to the workbench or hold it firmly and put a board under it. Remove the drill often, let it cool, and remove shavings; if the drill becomes too hot, it will get clogged with melted acrylic. If the piece of acrylic is heavy, say, over ¼-inch thick, it is a good idea to drill inward from both sides. To make large holes, start with a small bit; then enlarge the same hole by using a larger bit. The inside of the hole will be dull and frosty; but if you add turpentine or oil while drilling the hole, it will be clear.

Nails and screws applied directly to acrylic will shatter it, so a hole *must* be drilled first to accommodate the nail or screw. Make the hole somewhat larger than the diameter of the nail or screw you intend to use because acrylic expands or contracts under different temperatures. Remove drill slowly at the end of the drilling to avoid crazing when the drill emerges from the acrylic.

Cementing

Do not be misled by hardware-store dealers who tell you that most adhesives will bond acrylics. Generally they are not effective in cementing acrylic pieces; and some are water-soluble, which is hardly practical when you are making plant stands. You need a cement (available from suppliers), that actually becomes

After taping, cement pieces together with solvent and hypo applicator, brush or eyedropper. Sand surfaces to be cemented but do not polish. (Photo courtesy Rohm and Haas Co.)

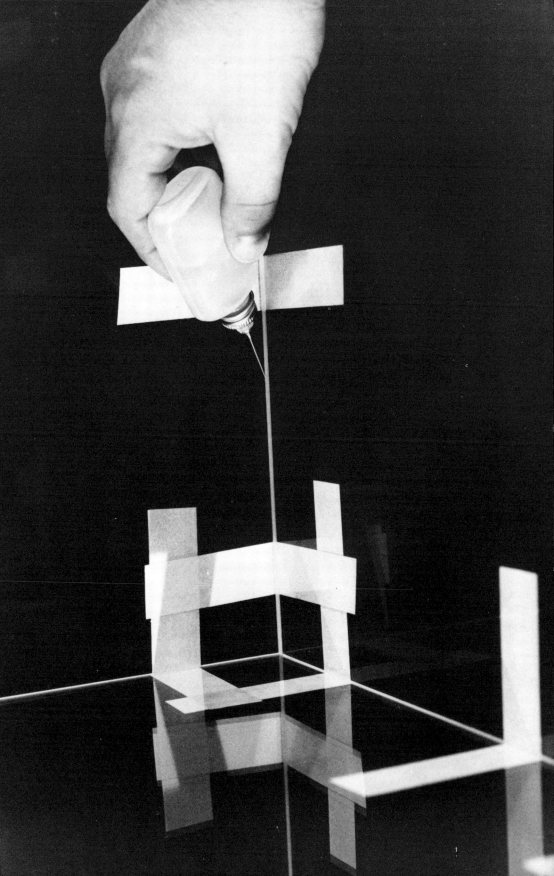

part of the acrylic when applied. The two cements to use are EDC (ethylene dichloride) and MDC (methylene dichloride). These are available from most acrylic suppliers.

The cementing process is simple. First carefully remove masking tape (the original protective coating). Sand surfaces to be cemented; do not polish. Mark material with red marking pencil where joining members are to be cemented. When holding pieces in place in preparation for cementing, use a draftsman's triangle against them to be sure of getting squareness. Apply the solvent cement with a small paintbrush or eyedropper where the pieces meet. The adhesive will flow between the areas of the pieces being cemented, soften them and, after a few minutes, harden and become part of the piece being cemented. Use light pressure for the first few seconds to bond the pieces; with time the bond becomes stronger.

Although for small projects it is possible to cement and hold pieces with your hands while they set, for larger ones the capillary method of cementing is better. Use masking tape to put together the cube or pedestal and then apply cement with an eyedropper or hypo-applicator (from dealers). Apply pressure, holding pieces for a few minutes. In a few hours remove the tape carefully. I have found that this method works better than holding pieces in place by hand while cementing. There is less room for error and the bond is much stronger, so by all means use the capillary method for larger pieces.

A good bond requires a flat surface, so never polish the edges of the plastic beforehand. It is best to cement plastics in warm (70° F.) rather than cool temperatures. See that there is adequate ventilation when using all cements, and do not get them in contact with skin or eyes under any circumstances. If you do, wash immediately.

If saw marks prevent you from bonding the pieces securely, use an 80-grit sandpaper until saw marks are removed and surfaces are parallel to each other. Remove protective coating for the cementing process. Work carefully and slowly.

When using cements for acrylics remember that these are toxic if inhaled for long periods of time, and of course, they should never be swallowed. Use in a well-ventilated place, away from children or pets.

Bending

When heated, acrylic becomes soft and pliable and can be folded or bent to almost any shape. When using bent acrylic, there is incredible latitude in making shelving and wall units, and the mechanics of hanging the units are much simpler than when working with glass or wood. Once the material cools, it remains rigid in its new shape.

There are many ways to bend acrylics in many shapes for the home do-it-yourselfer, but the simple line bend is all that needs to be mastered. For this, all you will need is a strip heater (from suppliers). This is a device that has an insulated heating element mounted in a frame.

To use the strip heater, remove the masking from the acrylic sheet; set the material on the heater and leave it in place until material is flexible enough to be formed. The strip heater will soften the line you want bent, allowing the remainder of the material to remain cool. The bend is made on the softened line, with the heated side of the material on the outside of the bend. Once bent, the heated acrylic must be secured in the shape to be formed. You can do this by either holding it in place by hand in the desired position until it cools, or by simply placing it taped to a mold or jig. Always wear flannel gloves when you are handling hot acrylics. (A jig can be made by gluing two pieces of wood together at a right angle.) The rate of cooling, whether held by hand or in a jig, depends upon the thickness of the acrylic and the room temperature. Generally it takes about 5 minutes.

Be sure the material is hot enough before you attempt to form it. If you try to form it before it is sufficiently heated, it will craze and become weakened. To determine when it is ready to be formed, observe: When it is like soft rubber to the touch it is ready to be formed.

Practice first with the strip heater on scraps of acrylic until you get the hang of it. This will give you an idea of how long it takes to reach forming temperature.

For safety, never leave a strip heater plugged in unattended, and do keep a small fire extinguisher on hand. Acrylic is flam-

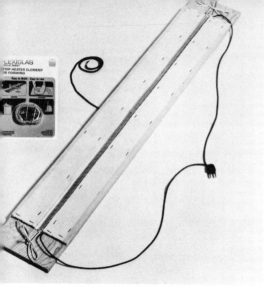

A strip heater will enable you to bend Plexiglas into many interesting shapes for plant shelves and stands.(Photo courtesy Rohm and Haas Co.)

mable. And one more thing: if you form a piece of acrylic and it is not to your liking, you can return it to its original flat shape by reheating it and then starting over.

Special tools and supplies for Plexiglas (the sheet acrylic made by Rohm and Haas) are available from Tools for Plexiglas, P.O. Box 14619, Philadelphia, Pa. 19134. Write for a free brochure.

Cleaning and Scratches

Do not clean acrylic or glass surfaces with scouring powders or kitchen cleansers or you will scratch the surfaces. Use carborundum powder (usually sold at hardware stores). Mix the powder with some water to form a paste, apply it to the acrylic or glass, let dry a few minutes and then polish with a soft cloth.

Remove stubborn stains such as grease or oil with kerosene or isopropyl alcohol; then wash surfaces with soap and water. Never use dirty or abrasive cloths on acrylics or you will scratch them. A light coating of wax such as Simoniz is fine protection for an acrylic surface and gives it a handsome sheen. Apply the wax with a soft cloth and then clean with cotton fabric.

As mentioned, acrylics do scratch, but if this happens, do not panic, because there are ways to erase the scratches. Using a 400-grit "wet or dry" sandpaper, sand the flaw lightly. Deeper scratches will need sanding and then buffing with a muslin wheel and fine-grit buffing compound.

3·Planter Designs and Construction

The design and construction of handcrafted plant accessories gives you a chance to work with your hands and, more importantly, to say "I made it myself." However, there are other advantages: You save money by making your own planters and stands, and you have the prerogative of choosing what you want, not what is available—which can be most important if you are filling certain space requirements. You do not have to make do; you can create a distinctive object—one of a kind and something to be proud of.

At this point you may say, "I know nothing about design or construction. I have never had any training in it." Hopefully this book will help you, and if you allow your need to dictate the design, you will have little trouble in creating a unique piece. As long as you can use a saw and drill and some sandpaper and cement, little more than common sense is needed.

Suit Design to Need

Design can be complicated or simple. For our purposes, most design is quite simple. For example, suppose you have a window where you would like some plants, but there is no sill—or if there is, you still do not want to just plunk pots on it. The answer is to design and construct shelving. Wrought-iron holders and shelves are available in kits, but they may not fit the space you have, and few are attractive. It is much better to design and make your own shelving from acrylic; it will look like a handsome part of the window rather than a tacked-on addition. You can use straight shelving, circular islands, or even triangular shelves. Let the window space tell you what suits the area best. If the room is severe, circular pads on suitable supports may be very attractive. If the window area is very small, straight shelves are your best answer. Where there is ample space, distinctive triangular shelving is indeed pleasant to see, and it will hold large pots.

As another example of suiting design to need, consider plant containers. Is the plant habit branching or cascading, rosette or upright? An upright plant needs a strong vertical unit, a rosette plant needs a wide base, and so on. Design accordingly. Working with acrylic or glass, you can build versatile cubical and cylindrical containers that will be much more attractive than the conventional round terra-cotta pots. Plant pedestals, too, can be shaped and formed to suit the character of the plant so that the pedestal and plant become one unit and complement each other. This is still another case of the design suiting the need. Working with plastic makes all this possible. In the following chapters we illustrate and tell you how to make many of these plant "pluses"; but first let us describe the basic shapes that can be made with acrylic.

Basic Shapes

THE CUBE

Once you learn to make the basic cube you can make one of any size because the construction is the same for all. The cube design is suitable for (1) hanging planters, (2) low pedestals, and (3) containers; so mastering cube construction is important because it will give you latitude for making many plant objects.

Accurately cut pieces of acrylic according to chart

Assemble cube using masking tape at edges

Note: Acrylic can be clear, tinted, opaque or mirrored

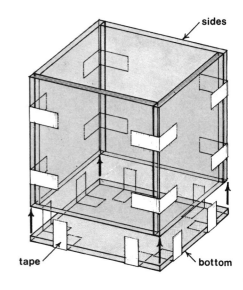

cube size	thickness	sides (4 req'd)	bottom
6"	$\frac{1}{8}$"	$6\frac{7}{8}$" sq.	6" sq.
12"	$\frac{1}{4}$"	$11\frac{3}{4}$" sq.	12" sq.
18"	$\frac{1}{2}$"	$17\frac{1}{2}$" sq.	18" sq.

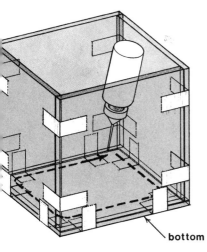

2

To cement, apply solvent along inside edges of bottom in a steady continuous motion

Use a solvent dispenser with a "needle nose" tip

Allow cube to sit 10 minutes

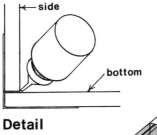

Detail

3

Lay cube on its side, then apply solvent to one of the lower inside edges

Allow to sit for 10 minutes

Turn cube to the next side & repeat

After all joints are cemented, allow cube to sit for 3 hours

Remove tape

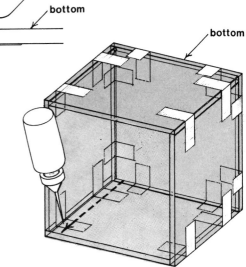

DRAWING: ADRIAN MARTINEZ

Capillary cementing – Cube planter

The cube, whatever size you choose, consists of five pieces. For example, a 12-inch cube takes one piece of 12 by 12-inch material, two pieces of 12 by 11¾, and two pieces of 11¾ by 12½. Assemble the cube by cementing in place one piece at a time; or first tape the cube together and then insert the cement along the edges with a narrow paintbrush or hypodermic needle; the cement will seep into and between the cut pieces and bond them. (See page 33.) Remember to allow 12 to 18 hours for the cement to set before planting the cube.

Cubes are easily made in a few minutes with acrylic sheet. You can use ⅛-inch acrylic for small containers; for larger ones use ¼-inch material. (Photo by Clark Photo/Graphic)

MATERIALS

USE CLEAR OR TINTED ¼" ACRYLIC

SIDES: 4 at 11¾" SQ., BUTT JOINTS

BOTTOM: 12" SQ., ADHERED TO BOTTOM OF SIDES

BASE: 4 at ¼" X ½" X 11", ADHERED TO BOTTOM

NOTE: TO STACK, BASE FITS INTO OPENING OF LOWER CUBE

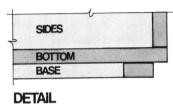

DETAIL

Stacking Plant Cubes

DRAWING: ADRIAN MARTINEZ

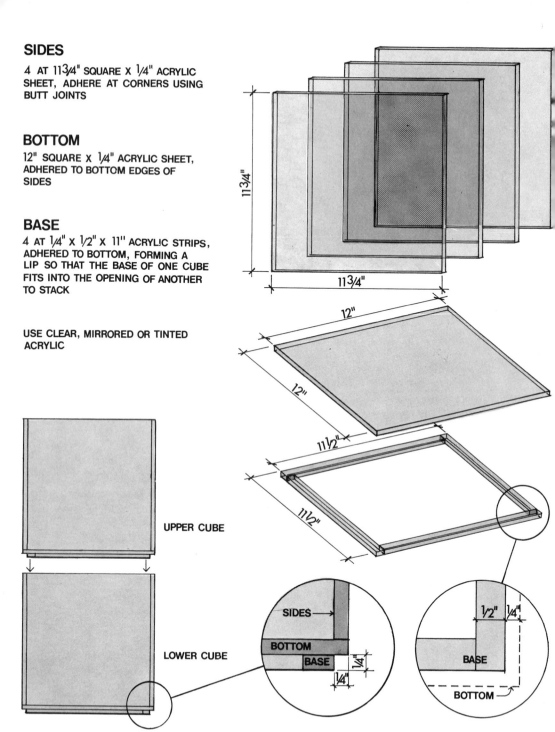

SIDES

4 AT 11 3/4" SQUARE X 1/4" ACRYLIC
SHEET, ADHERE AT CORNERS USING
BUTT JOINTS

BOTTOM

12" SQUARE X 1/4" ACRYLIC SHEET,
ADHERED TO BOTTOM EDGES OF
SIDES

BASE

4 AT 1/4" X 1/2" X 11" ACRYLIC STRIPS,
ADHERED TO BOTTOM, FORMING A
LIP SO THAT THE BASE OF ONE CUBE
FITS INTO THE OPENING OF ANOTHER
TO STACK

USE CLEAR, MIRRORED OR TINTED
ACRYLIC

11 3/4"

11 3/4"

12"

12"

11 1/2"

11 1/2"

UPPER CUBE

LOWER CUBE

SECTION

DETAIL

SIDES

BOTTOM

BASE

1/4"

1/4"

DETAIL

1/2"   1/4"

BASE

BOTTOM

Stacking Plant Cube Construction

DRAWING: ADRIAN MARTINEZ

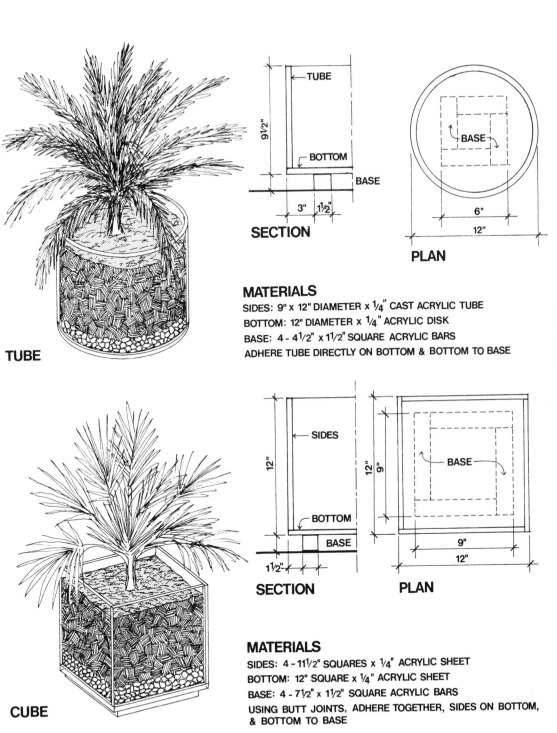

TUBE

SECTION

9½"

← TUBE

← BOTTOM

BASE

3" 1½"

PLAN

BASE

6"

12"

MATERIALS
SIDES: 9" x 12" DIAMETER x ¼" CAST ACRYLIC TUBE
BOTTOM: 12" DIAMETER x ¼" ACRYLIC DISK
BASE: 4 - 4½" x 1½" SQUARE ACRYLIC BARS
ADHERE TUBE DIRECTLY ON BOTTOM & BOTTOM TO BASE

CUBE

SECTION

12"

1½"

← SIDES

← BOTTOM

BASE

PLAN

12"
9"

BASE

9"

12"

MATERIALS
SIDES: 4 - 11½" SQUARES x ¼" ACRYLIC SHEET
BOTTOM: 12" SQUARE x ¼" ACRYLIC SHEET
BASE: 4 - 7½" x 1½" SQUARE ACRYLIC BARS
USING BUTT JOINTS, ADHERE TOGETHER, SIDES ON BOTTOM,
& BOTTOM TO BASE

Acrylic Planters

DRAWING: ADRIAN MARTINEZ

You can use several cubes in a modular setup to make a handsome plant grouping. Some cubes can be used as pedestals, and others can be planted for display. Using handsome mirror acrylic sheets is still another way of creating a really different look. You can also use colored acrylic to brighten a room and blend with furnishings. The cubes are movable, so you can create an endless array of plant-furniture designs. Mix and match is the motto here, as the modular plant arrangements can be used in limitless combinations to suit your own tastes.

THE CYLINDER (TUBE)

Wherever you need a softening touch in a room, use the cylinder rather than the strong vertical lines of the cube. By mastering the construction of a cylinder you can make one of any size. The construction is as simple as making the cube; have the cylinder (tube), cut to length by your supplier, and then cement a disk at one end for a bottom.

You can use a single cylinder as either a "sitting" or hanging plant container, or use three cylinders of various heights to make

Cylinders of acrylic create an interesting plant group suitable for almost any room. (Photo by Clark Photo/Graphic)

MATERIALS

USE 1/8" THICK ACRYLIC TUBES

SIDES: 1 at 4" DIA. X 3" HIGH

    1 at 3 1/2" DIA. X 3 1/2" HIGH

    1 at 3" DIA. X 4" HIGH

BOTTOMS: 3 - 1/8" THICK DISKS, AT SAME DIAMETER

        AS TUBES

ADHERE BOTTOMS TO TUBES, GROUP TOGETHER &

ADHERE AT POINTS WHERE THEY TOUCH TO FORM

A SINGLE UNIT

3 1/2" DIA.

3" DIA.

4" DIA.

TOP VIEW

Small Tubular Planter

DRAWING: ADRIAN MARTINEZ

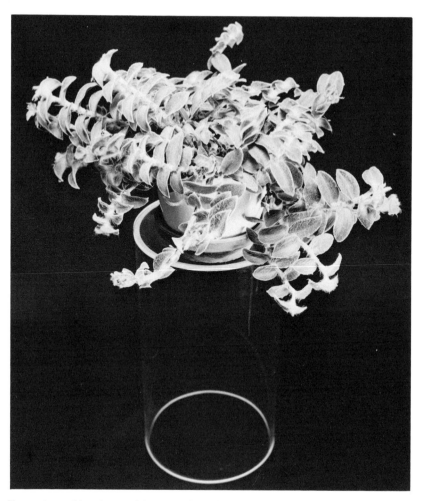

Turned upside down this container becomes a pedestal to display a lovely cyanotis plant. (Photo by Clark Photo/Graphic)

An acrylic cylinder with a bottom makes an excellent container for a plant. This is miniature bamboo. (Photo by Clark Photo/Graphic)

a grouping for plants. The cylinder can also be a pedestal for a plant. Measure the diameter of the clay or glazed pot just below the rim. Select a ¼-inch-thick acrylic cylinder of the same size and, as though it were a sleeve, insert the clay pot into it. The rim will hold the pot in place. There is a definite advantage in this arrangement: The cylinder gathers moisture after you water the plants and thus creates additional humidity for the well-being of the plant.

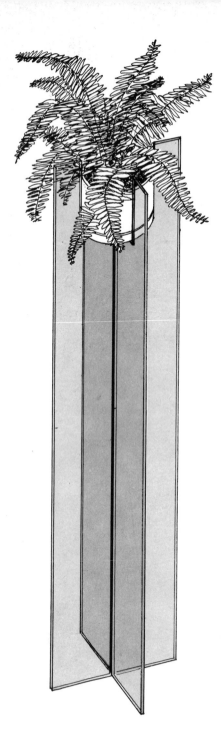

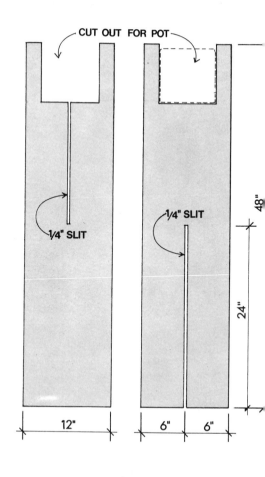

CUT OUT FOR POT

1/4" SLIT

1/4" SLIT

48"

24"

12"

6" 6"

MATERIALS

2 – 1' X 4' X 1/4" TINTED ACRYLIC SHEETS
CUTOUTS AT TOP TO CRADLE POT SNUGLY
1/4" WIDE SLITS FOR CENTER LAP JOINT, ADHESIVE
NOT NECESSARY

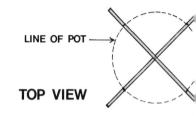

LINE OF POT →

TOP VIEW

Interlocking Plant Stand

DRAWING: ADRIAN MARTINE.

This terrarium was built in fifteen minutes using seven pieces of acrylic with a central, diagonal divider. The seventh (top piece) is not shown. (Photo by Clark Photo/Graphic)

THE RECTANGLE

The rectangle is generally used as a plant pedestal or container and may be 12 to 60 inches tall, depending upon your room and what kind of plant you are using. You can also group several rectangles of varying heights to create a stair-step design. Cascading plants are most suited for pedestals, although upright or rosette plants like ferns are fine too.

The rectangular pedestal is simple to construct and involves five pieces of acrylic; it is actually an elongated cube. Basically it is constructed in the same manner as a cube.

A more elaborate pedestal can be made with six pieces of acrylic; for example, with 10 by 10 by 36-inch material of ¼-inch thickness. For this you need two pieces of 10 by 10-inch acrylic, two pieces of 10 by 36 inches, and two pieces of 9½ by 36. This design provides the pedestal with a plant pocket and gives you a very unique piece of plant furniture. *Note:* Try this design only after you have mastered the cube because it is somewhat more difficult and you need more experience to do it well.

43

TOP

12″

12″

9″

20″

1/4″ holes

SIDE

MATERIALS

SIDES: 3 - 20″× 12″×1/4″ ACRYLIC SHEETS
BOTTOM: 12″ EQUILATERAL TRIANGLE OF 1/4″ ACRYLIC SHEET
WITH 14 DRAINAGE HOLES

NOTE

USING BUTT JOINTS, ADHERE 2 SIDES WITH BOTTOM PLATFORM,
SECURE THIRD SIDE IN PLACE.
CUT SIDE EDGES AT 60° BEVEL.
BOND JOINTS WITH EPOXY.

DRAWING: JAMES CAREW

Triangular Acrylic Planter

THE TRIANGLE

You will not find triangular containers at nurseries but it is easy to design these special containers yourself. Basically the construction is the same as for cubical and rectangular containers except that the triangular ones are somewhat more complex. Three sides are cemented to a triangular base, and the places where the sides meet—called a butt joint—must be chamfered (angled) to fit snugly. You can file the edges yourself but it is difficult, so ask your plastic dealer if he can do the edgework for you.

Triangular plant pedestals are also possible. Cement three triangular sides of acrylic sheet to each other, and then cement the top and bottom triangle in place. This is an effective corner accent and well suited to many rooms. These units can also be used in groups to make different modular arrangements.

U OR L SHAPES

With the aid of the strip heater (see Chapter 2) you can make L-shaped shelves to hold plants or U-shaped units to form two shelves. These small units are very attractive with greenery anywhere in a room and add that necessary spot of color. On transparent shelving the plants seem to float; this is another advantage, because they are extremely appealing.

To make these shelves, make a mark on the acrylic where you want the bend, and then, using the strip heater, form the material to the desired shape. A 3-inch-diameter curve works very well for, say, an 18-inch shelf. This gives space for two or three plants to a shelf or four to six plants to a unit.

For attaching the units to a wall you will have to drill holes in the flat side of the acrylic; make them larger than the diameter of the screw. The U-shaped shelf can also be used vertically rather than horizontally. For a vertical shelf, cement in place two pieces of flat acrylic for shelving. (See pages 46–47 for illustrations.)

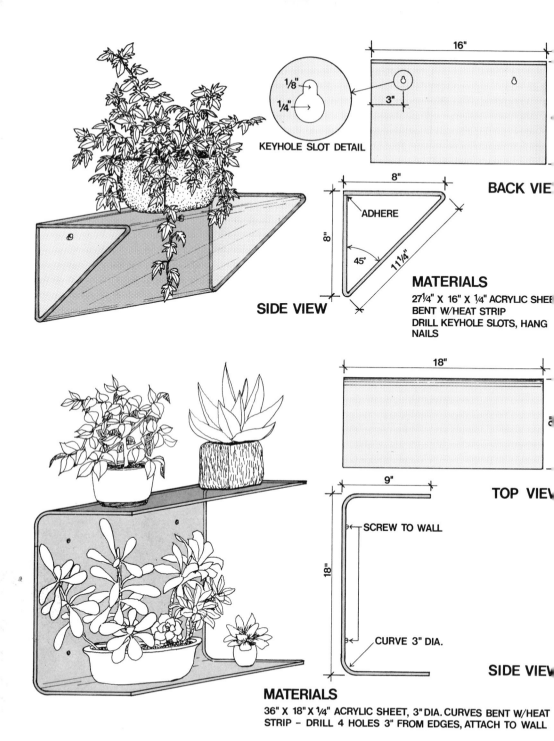

KEYHOLE SLOT DETAIL

1/8"
1/4"

16"

3"

BACK VIE

8"

ADHERE

8"

45°

11 1/4"

SIDE VIEW

MATERIALS

27 1/4" X 16" X 1/4" ACRYLIC SHEE
BENT W/HEAT STRIP
DRILL KEYHOLE SLOTS, HANG
NAILS

18"

TOP VIEW

9"

SCREW TO WALL

18"

CURVE 3" DIA.

SIDE VIEW

MATERIALS

36" X 18" X 1/4" ACRYLIC SHEET, 3" DIA. CURVES BENT W/HEAT
STRIP – DRILL 4 HOLES 3" FROM EDGES, ATTACH TO WALL

Wall Mounted Plant Shelves DRAWING: ADRIAN MARTINE

Made by using a strip heater, these Plexiglas shelves provide a functional and handsome place for plants. The lip keeps plants from falling
and sunlight reaches all plants because of the transparency of the material. (Photo courtesy Rohm and Haas Co.)

4·Terrariums

Today, because of improved plastics, acrylic, specifically, a terrarium does not have to be a rectangularly shaped glass aquarium with metal supports. By using new epoxies with acrylic you can fashion miniature greenhouses in various designs. A unique cylindrical garden made from an acrylic tube is only one possibility. There are dozens, and what you select depends upon the design and just how much money you want to invest. With commercially made plastic terrariums, you are limited to a few designs, but with acrylic, a few tools and cement you can make almost any design you want and thus create an individual rather than a common piece.

Terrariums can be made in a multitude of shapes, sizes, and designs limited only by your imagination and the allotted space. Note that you must balance the scale of the terrarium to the space it will occupy. For example, a 10-inch acrylic garden on a 5-foot coffee table simply will not work; a larger one will. Ideal sizes for variously shaped terrariums are:

10″ x 10″ (square)
12″ x 16″ (rectangle)
6″ x 6″ (hexagon)

Looking down into the terrarium. Note the divider that separates the desert environment from the tropical habitat. (Photo by Clark Photo/-Graphic)

For cylindrical terrariums use ¼-inch-thick acrylic in a 10- or 12-inch-tube size.

You must also make sure the terrarium has ample planting space to ensure a good balance of light, air, temperature and soil. These are the prime requirements of a terrarium. Balance of all elements—plants, soil, air, moisture—is the key that keeps terrarium plants healthy.

Making the Terrarium

As previously mentioned, when using acrylic sheet it is best to buy precut sizes rather than large sheets that you yourself must cut. This eliminates the need for tools and exact cutting, and the cost is not much more. Basically, the terrarium can be just four sides cemented to a bottom panel, with a removable panel for a top.

A more sophisticated flat-sheet terrarium is a 12-inch cube set on a plywood pedestal. A galvanized metal tray is used as an insert between the pedestal and the terrarium. This elegant unit elevates the garden and is extremely handsome, although, of course, it costs more than a conventional terrarium.

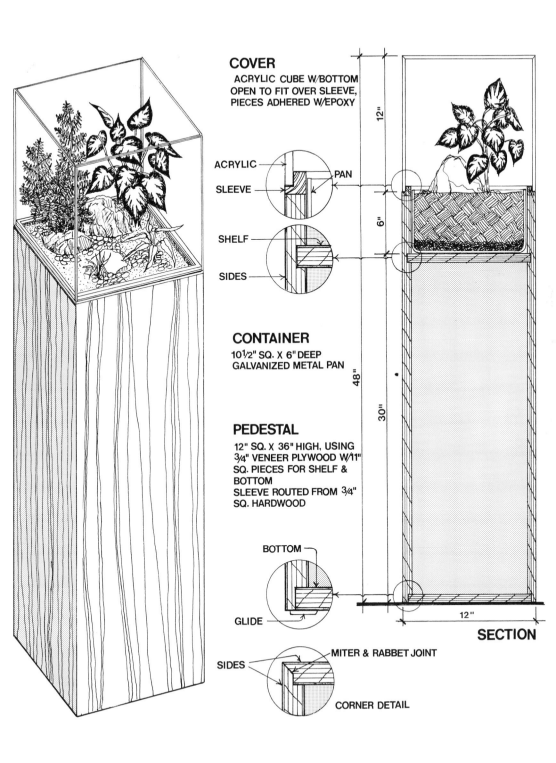

COVER
ACRYLIC CUBE W/BOTTOM OPEN TO FIT OVER SLEEVE, PIECES ADHERED W/EPOXY

ACRYLIC
SLEEVE
PAN

SHELF

SIDES

12"

6"

CONTAINER
10½" SQ. X 6" DEEP
GALVANIZED METAL PAN

48"

30"

PEDESTAL
12" SQ. X 36" HIGH, USING
¾" VENEER PLYWOOD W/11"
SQ. PIECES FOR SHELF &
BOTTOM
SLEEVE ROUTED FROM ¾"
SQ. HARDWOOD

BOTTOM

GLIDE

12"

SECTION

MITER & RABBET JOINT

SIDES

CORNER DETAIL

Pedestal Terrarium

DRAWING: ADRIAN MARTINEZ

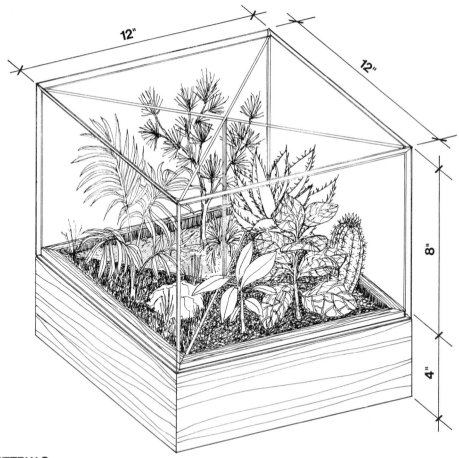

MATERIALS

COVER TOP & SIDES: 1/4" ACRYLIC SHEET, MITERED JOINTS, REMOVABLE TOP

DIAGONAL DIVIDERS: 1/8" ACRYLIC SHEET, LAP-JOINTED AT CENTER, FIXED TO BOTTOM

BASE SIDES: 3/4" WOOD, WATERPROOFED, MITERED JOINTS, TOP EDGE RABBETED FOR COVER

BASE BOTTOM: 1/2" EXTERIOR PLYWOOD DADOED INTO SIDES

NOTE: DIVISIONS ALLOW FOR FOUR "CLIMATIC" PLANT ENVIRONMENTS

Acrylic & Wood Terrarium   DRAWING: ADRIAN MARTINEZ

A variation of the rectangular terrarium is the compartmented design. Use four pieces of flat acrylic crisscrossed, with four sides to enclose the case. After the unit is cemented, construct a suitable base of redwood. Here, too, as in the pedestal terrarium, you might want to insert a galvanized tray into the wood base.

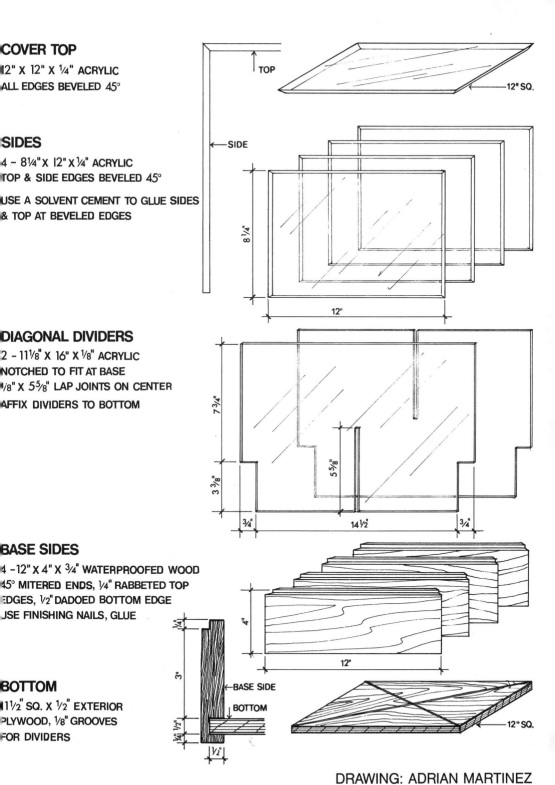

COVER TOP

12" X 12" X 1/4" ACRYLIC
ALL EDGES BEVELED 45°

SIDES

4 – 8 1/4" X 12" X 1/4" ACRYLIC
TOP & SIDE EDGES BEVELED 45°

USE A SOLVENT CEMENT TO GLUE SIDES & TOP AT BEVELED EDGES

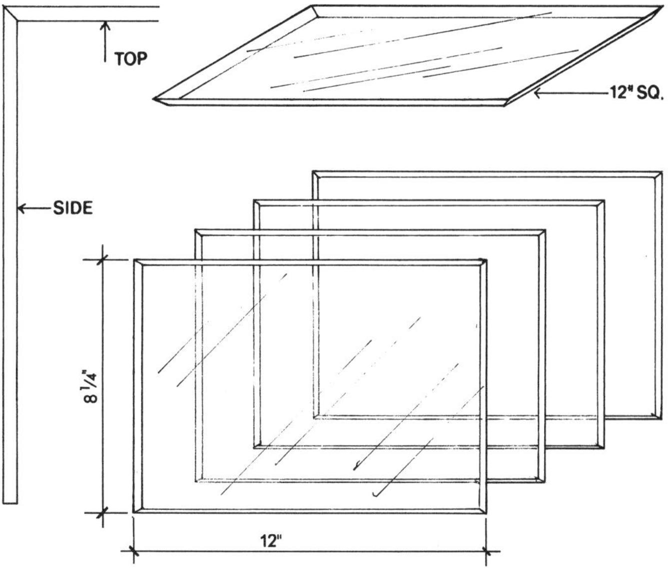

TOP
12" SQ.
SIDE
8 1/4
12"

DIAGONAL DIVIDERS

2 – 11 1/8" X 16" X 1/8" ACRYLIC
NOTCHED TO FIT AT BASE
1/8" X 5 5/8" LAP JOINTS ON CENTER
AFFIX DIVIDERS TO BOTTOM

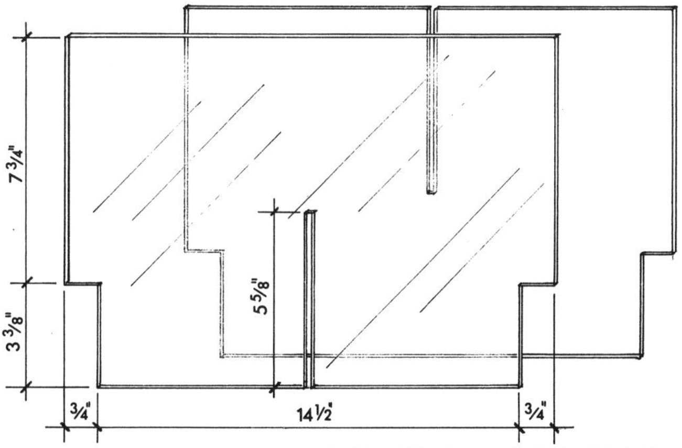

7 3/4"
3 3/8"
5 5/8"
3/4"
14 1/2"
3/4"

BASE SIDES

4 – 12" X 4" X 3/4" WATERPROOFED WOOD
45° MITERED ENDS, 1/4" RABBETED TOP EDGES, 1/2" DADOED BOTTOM EDGE
USE FINISHING NAILS, GLUE

BOTTOM

11 1/2" SQ. X 1/2" EXTERIOR PLYWOOD, 1/8" GROOVES FOR DIVIDERS

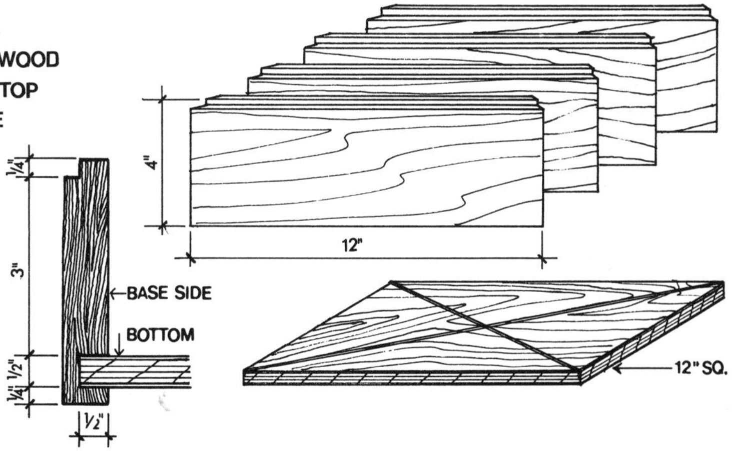

4"
12"
1/4"
3"
1/2"
1/4"
1/2"
BASE SIDE
BOTTOM
12" SQ.

DRAWING: ADRIAN MARTINEZ

Acrylic & Wood Terrarium Construction

This terrarium is a Plexiglas square set atop a plastic base; another easy-to-make project. (Photo courtesy Rohm and Haas Co.)

The rectangular and cube terrariums take some time to make, but cylindrical ones can be assembled in 10 minutes. Buy the ¼-inch tubes precut to size, and use disks for bottom and top. All you do for this terrarium is cement one disk to the bottom and set the other disk on top, and you are ready to plant. And if you grow tired of the terrarium, you can always disassemble it, turn the tube upside down, and use it as a plant pedestal. Versatility is one of the wonders of acrylic!

When we think of terrariums we naturally think of them in a vertical position, but with acrylic tubes it is quite easy to make a horizontal greenery too—and these are distinctive pieces. You cannot find anything like them at stores. Simply cement half disks to each end of a tube, and then place the terrarium horizontally on a wooden base (sold at hobby shops), or, simpler yet, find a suitable long dish, fill it with sand, and merely place the terrarium in position.

Here an acrylic rectangle is used on a wooden base. It makes a lovely greenery for table or desk. (Photo by Clark Photo/Graphic)

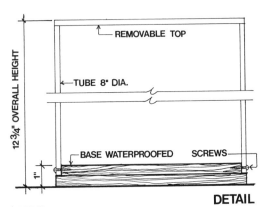

REMOVABLE TOP

12³⁄₄" OVERALL HEIGHT

TUBE 8" DIA.

BASE WATERPROOFED   SCREWS

1"

DETAIL

VERTICAL TERRARIUM

MATERIALS

VERTICAL TERRARIUM
TOP: 8" DIA. x 1/4" ACRYLIC DISK
SIDES: 8" DIA. x 12" HIGH x 1/4" ACRYLIC TUBE
BASE: 7 1/2" & 8" DIA. x 1/2" REDWOOD DISKS ADHERED TO EACH
        OTHER TO FORM A LIP FOR THE TUBE, ATTACH W/SCREWS

HORIZONTAL TERRARIUM
SIDES: 10" DIA. x 16" LONG x 1/4" ACRYLIC TUBE
BASE : 2 - 2 1/2" x 8" x 1/2" ACRYLIC PIECES W/CUTOUTS FOR TUBE
      TO SIT ON, ADHERED AT ENDS
ENDS: 2 - 9 1/2" DIA. x 1/4" ACRYLIC DISKS (1 CUT IN HALF)
      ONLY THE UPPER HALF DISK AT ONE END IS TO
      BE REMOVABLE & HELD IN PLACE W 1/2" NAILS IN PRE-
      DRILLED HOLES

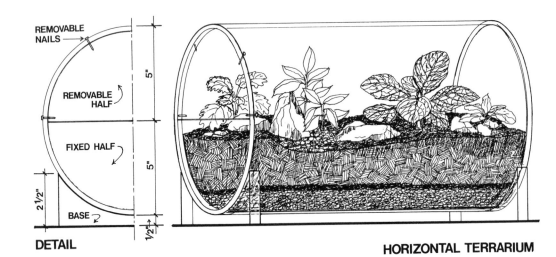

REMOVABLE
NAILS

5"

REMOVABLE
HALF

FIXED HALF

5"

2 1/2"

BASE

1/2"

DETAIL

HORIZONTAL TERRARIUM

Acrylic Tube Terrariums

DRAWING: ADRIAN MARTINEZ

You can also try hexagonal terrariums, with six panels cemented together. However, end cuts must be chamfered so panels butt together flush when they are cemented. Precision is absolutely necessary when assembling this unit, so tackle it only after you have become somewhat experienced in working with acrylic. (See drawing page 58.)

Terrariums in the Air

Hanging plants are popular and so are hanging terrariums. They are excellent decorative accents, and it takes only a few minutes to prepare a hanging planter. Simply drill four holes, one in each corner of the cube or rectangular terrarium and suspend it with hooks and wire from the ceiling.

The cylindrical terrarium can be treated the same way, and I have found that you can even sidestep the hole-drilling in the horizontal cylindrical greenery by passing a 2-inch-diameter acrylic rod through the cylinder and then suspending the rod on suitable supports. Use eye hooks for drilled holes and monofilament wire from the hooks to support the garden. Use a heavy eye bolt in the ceiling.

You can also elevate desk and table terrariums on acrylic or wooden stands. Besides lifting the garden off the table surface and preventing water stains, the stand puts the case in a better position to be seen and appreciated.

Miniature Greenhouses

These units are available commercially, but it is so easy to make your own and so much cheaper. Simply construct a box design; take the rectangular terrarium and put a roof on it. This will mean two more pieces of acrylic for the eaves and two triangles to complete the greenhouse. In this greenery you can grow almost any kind of plant you want, and you can also propagate plants because of the fine humidity inside.

The acrylic greenhouse is delightful in small sizes on a table

MATERIALS

USE CLEAR ¼" ACRYLIC

TOP: HEXAGONAL, 9" EACH SIDE,
    POLISHED EDGES

SIDES: 6 at 9" x 16", SIDE EDGES
BEVELED 30°, TOP EDGE POLISHED

DIVIDER: 6" x 17", SLIPPED IN
DIAGONALLY

BASE: 2 HEXAGONS, ONE 9" THE OTHER
8⅝" EACH SIDE, ADHERED FORMING
A LIP FOR THE BOTTOM EDGE OF SIDES

NOTE: USE A SOLVENT CEMENT TO
GLUE SIDES TOGETHER & TO BASE

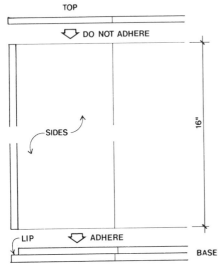

TOP

⬇ DO NOT ADHERE

SIDES

16"

LIP   ⬇ ADHERE

BASE

SECTION

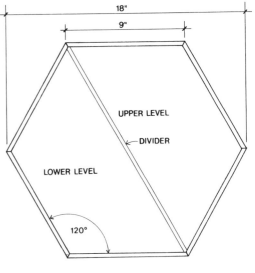

18"

9"

UPPER LEVEL

← DIVIDER

LOWER LEVEL

120°

PLAN

Hexagonal Terrarium

DRAWING: ADRIAN MARTINEZ

A miniature greenhouse has been made from Plexiglas sheet and can be used outdoors or indoors as well to start seeds and establish seedlings. The unit is made from six pieces of Plexiglas on a wooden base. (Photo courtesy Rohm and Haas Co.)

or desk, and, as I have recently seen, it is becoming increasingly popular in much larger sizes outdoors.

Planting the Terrarium

Assembling the acrylic terrarium is simple, and so is its planting. The main consideration is that the garden should simulate a natural scene; thus a hilly terrarium looks best. It reflects a natural environment and suggests a miniature woodland, desert, or whatever scene you choose.

Make hills and valleys, inserting appropriate small rocks and ledges to give the natural look. Select small- and medium-sized plants that are in scale with the case from the many fine plants available (see Chapter 7). To plant the terrarium, pour in a 1-inch bed of gravel and then a 3- to 4-inch soil bed with some charcoal chips. Now make your terrarium. Make planting holes and insert the larger plants in the rear and the smaller ones toward the front. Plant in an arc arrangement so there is viewing space at the front. Rather than using one plant in an area, group several together to create a picture, and then balance the terrarium by repeating the same plant or plants in some other area.

Once plants are in place you may feel there is something missing because bare areas of soil show. Use ground cover plants to clothe the soil in emerald green and make the scene look like a miniature forest. Or place rocks and stones appropriately and you will strengthen the effect of a desert scene.

For the first few days, observe your terrarium, and if too much moisture condenses on the sides, remove a few plants and lift the cover a few hours a day. Occasionally shake the lid so excess water falls into the garden. Keep these miniature greeneries out of sun but in good light; sunlight will quickly heat the case and bake plants.

Cleaning and Maintaining Terrariums

Clean your terrarium occasionally, both inside and out. You want to keep the garden clean and beautiful, and it takes only a few seconds to make things sparkling. Use a damp cloth to remove dust and film from surfaces, and give special attention to the soil line against the acrylic, where accumulated salts may stain surfaces.

Plants in terrariums will need grooming and trimming to keep them at their best. Remove dead or decaying leaves as soon as you see them, and prune plants that are getting too large for the container. Cutting away small pieces of plants will not harm them and may even encourage new growth.

5·Containers

Making your own acrylic containers provides you with great flexibility in design and size. And once the basic design principles are understood, you can practically make any kind of planter; you are not limited just to circular shapes. (The construction of the large cube and cylindrical container is fully covered in Chapter 3.)

Acrylic containers have several design pluses. There are so many commercial containers for plants on the market that it may seem ridiculous to make your own. But often the commercial pots and tubs lack good design. And many times you want a container to suit a certain location—a custom unit. With acrylics you can make what you *want* and not what you have to buy. There is also a cultural plus to using acrylic containers: soil does not dry out as quickly as in terra-cotta pots, so you do not have to water the plants as much.

Acrylic is transparent and allows for a unique view of growing plants. Roots and soil create interesting designs, and there is a sleek contemporary character about acrylic containers that complements foliage in almost any room setting.

A small rectangular container, say, 6 inches high, 10 or 12 inches long and 4 inches wide, has many uses for plants; yet at the moment there is no commercially made unit of this kind on the market. This setup can be made from five pieces of acrylic sheet (four sides and a bottom) to accommodate bulbs and small low-growing plants. It is highly effective on a windowsill or shelf, small but pretty, and worth the small cost.

Another ideal container is a rectangular box set on edge, measuring 4 by 4 inches for the base, with sides about 10 inches tall. This is another setting for small house plants, and it fits into awkward spaces. I have made these units for shelf or windowsills, but they can also be used on small tables and desks for a spot of decoration; in mirrored acrylic they are beautiful.

The construction for either container is relatively simple. Cut sides and bottom and cement them together. This basic construction holds true for large boxes (for medium- and large-sized plants): simply cement four sides to a bottom.

Plant the acrylic containers carefully and neatly, because what is inside can be seen from the outside. First use a layer of pea gravel, followed by a layer of charcoal, and then add the soil for the plant.

Hanging Planters

In 1970, when I wrote my book "Hanging Gardens," there were few suitable commercial hanging containers available. (Quite frankly, there are still few satisfactory commercially made hanging planters, although I am sure we shall see better units in the future.) At first I used wire baskets—old favorites—which worked very well. However, they had serious drawbacks. They could not be used indoors because excess water drained out and stained the floors. The alternative was to move plants to the sink each time for watering—hardly a pleasant chore. Furthermore, they were not suited to most indoor settings.

I decided to design some type of hanging planter. I used terracotta pots and added handcrafted trays attached to the bottom. I

This plant helper can be used as a window box or a hanging planter. It is made from ¼-inch acrylic sheet with two hole cutouts to accommodate pots. The inside of the planter has gravel to catch excess water and help create humidity for the plants. (Photo by author)

Using a cylinder with half-moon sides, you can create an interesting hanging planter. The planter is held by a solid acrylic rod. (Photo by Clark Photo/Graphic)

also made acrylic containers with a compartmented bottom. The acrylic planters looked lovely in my living and dining rooms, and it was easy to move these hanging containers because they were not so heavy as standard pots. I also discovered that by making my own acrylic hanging containers I could assemble any size I wanted, and it was an opportunity to let the plant dictate the container rather than the other way around.

As mentioned in Chapter 4, hanging terrariums are easy to make. And these same cylinders can be used for potted plants. You can set a clay or plastic saucer that fits the diameter of the tube into the container, fill with gravel, and place a potted plant in it. If the idea of seeing the pot through the plastic bothers you, wedge sphagnum moss between the pot and the acrylic container. Using plants this way is the sleeve-within-a-sleeve method. You can also plant directly into the acrylic container, whether it is square or round.

Another excellent hanging unit for plants can be made from a rectangular acrylic box (four sides, a bottom and a top), with two round cutouts for the pots. The pot rims rest in the holes and drain into the platform, which can be filled with gravel.

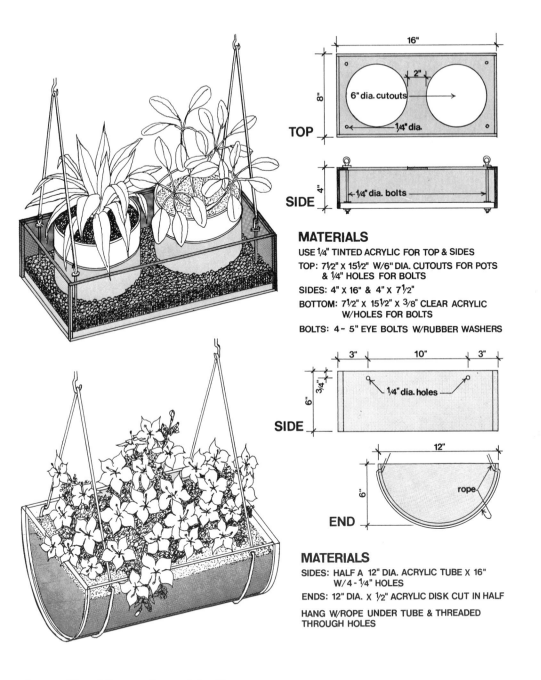

TOP

16"

8"

6" dia. cutouts

2"

¼" dia.

SIDE

4"

¼" dia. bolts

MATERIALS

USE ¼" TINTED ACRYLIC FOR TOP & SIDES

TOP: 7½" x 15½" W/6" DIA. CUTOUTS FOR POTS & ¼" HOLES FOR BOLTS

SIDES: 4" x 16" & 4" x 7½"

BOTTOM: 7½" x 15½" x ⅜" CLEAR ACRYLIC W/HOLES FOR BOLTS

BOLTS: 4 – 5" EYE BOLTS W/RUBBER WASHERS

SIDE

3" · 10" · 3"

6"

¾"

¼" dia. holes

END

12"

6"

rope

MATERIALS

SIDES: HALF A 12" DIA. ACRYLIC TUBE X 16" W/ 4 - ¼" HOLES

ENDS: 12" DIA. X ½" ACRYLIC DISK CUT IN HALF

HANG W/ROPE UNDER TUBE & THREADED THROUGH HOLES

Acrylic Hanging Units

DRAWING: ADRIAN MARTINEZ

Circles of ¼-inch acrylic are used to provide hanging platforms for plants strung together with mono-filament wire. Circles can be large or small, depending on plants used. (Photo by author)

Occasionally excess·water will have to be removed, so insert a layer of fine marble chips in the bottom of the box so the water can evaporate and provide humidity for plants. String wires in predrilled holes at the edges so you can hang the unit.

This is really an excellent container for hanging plants because air can reach the bottoms of the pots and the gravel bed looks attractive. I have mainly used terra-cotta pots in my hanging gardens, but recently clear plastic pots have appeared at nurseries, and although somewhat expensive, they are very effective when used in these units.

You can also make square-shaped planters using five pieces of acrylic cemented together with epoxy. Drill side holes at the top of the box to run wire supports for ceiling hooks.

Not really a hanging container itself is a unique innovation that I call a disk hanger; the potted plant is placed on this. An attractive setting for hanging plants can be made in a few minutes. Order precut circles (disks) from your supplier. If you have small potted plants, buy 4- or 6-inch-diameter circles; larger plants will need appropriately larger circles.

You can make two- or three-shelved suspended hangers in the following way: Drill four ¼-inch holes in each circle. String monofilament wire through the holes to hold disks (like a hammock). Knot the top of the wire through screw eyes in the wall.

With these units, each circle will hold one potted plant, and from a distance the plant will seem to float in air. If you use three circles as a unit, you can create a column of floating greenery that is an asset in any room.

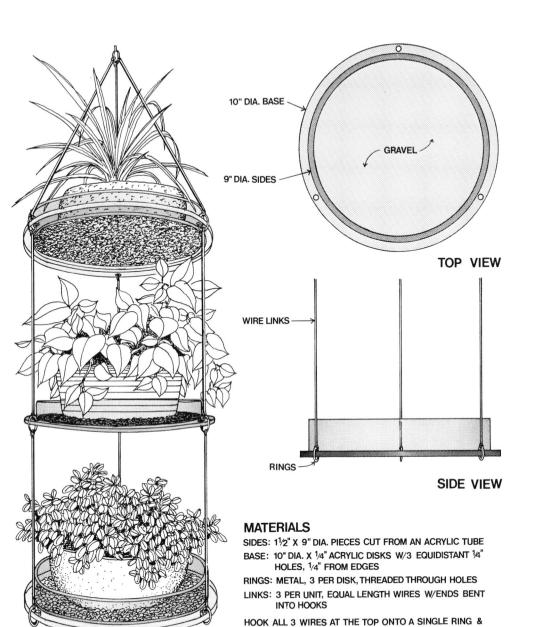

10" DIA. BASE

9" DIA. SIDES

GRAVEL

TOP VIEW

WIRE LINKS

RINGS

SIDE VIEW

MATERIALS

SIDES: 1½" X 9" DIA. PIECES CUT FROM AN ACRYLIC TUBE

BASE: 10" DIA. X ¼" ACRYLIC DISKS W/3 EQUIDISTANT ¼"
HOLES, ¼" FROM EDGES

RINGS: METAL, 3 PER DISK, THREADED THROUGH HOLES

LINKS: 3 PER UNIT, EQUAL LENGTH WIRES W/ENDS BENT
INTO HOOKS

HOOK ALL 3 WIRES AT THE TOP ONTO A SINGLE RING &
SUSPEND

Suspended Trays

DRAWING: ADRIAN MARTINEZ

HOW TO PLANT HANGING CONTAINERS

The procedure for planting see-through hanging containers is somewhat different from planting terra-cotta pots. These containers will usually have no drainage holes. Careful preparation of the planting bed is necessary so you do not end up with a sour soil. Insert a layer of fine pea gravel, about 1 inch for a 6-inch pot. Sprinkle in charcoal chips to keep the soil sweet, and then add a mound of soil. Center the plant, and fill in and around with soil to within 1 inch of the top of the pot. Press soil down firmly to eliminate air pockets. For a good display, place the plants around the perimeter of a round container (use three or four plants). In a square-shaped planter, put the plants at the back and allow the front to be open; plants will fill in nicely once they start growing. (See Chapter 7 for plants for hanging gardens.)

Floor Planters

The basic construction for cube, cylinder, rectangular and triangular containers is explained in Chapter 3. The floor planter is generally large, say, 8 to 10 inches in diameter or 8 to 10 inches square. It can be used by itself as a room accent; or where there is space you can use a group of three cylinders for greenery. Or you can use modular units, that is, squares or cubes arranged as you wish to fill a room corner, to add dimension, to guide traffic through a room, or as green islands in a room. There is amazing versatility in using acrylic floor planters, and you can place them in almost any room in the home because acrylics blend well with most decors. The clear crystal appearance is handsome, and, as mentioned, you can also use colored or mirrored acrylic for stunning effects.

With large floor planters it is a good idea to provide some kind of drainage facility. You can do this as follows: Insert a dummy shelf with four drain holes in the box. This can be cemented in place, using acrylic rods as supports. Fill the planter with a 1- to 2-inch bed of gravel, and then place the drain hole board on

1. Cement rods to bottom disk

2. Insert 2″ gravel bed

3. Insert drainage disk

4. Add soil and pot plant

DRAWING: JAMES CAREW

Acrylic Planter with Drain Board

A square Plexiglas container is used as a hanging decorative accent suspended from ceiling with handsome rope. (Photo courtesy Rohm and Haas Co.)

top of this on the rods. Now you can plant directly into the box, or merely slip a potted plant in place.

When you repot floor planters you will have to use a different method than for standard clay or glazed pots. This is the way to do it: Dig out topsoil carefully so as not to scratch acrylic, first letting the soil dry out somewhat. Now, grasping the crown of the plant with your hand, jiggle it slightly and keep moving it back and forth until it comes loose. Hopefully, the plant will come out with some of the root ball intact. Put the plant on its side. Now turn over the acrylic planter, and with the palm of your hand knock the outside to loosen all soil. Repeat this process until all soil is removed. Then wash the container thoroughly with soap and water to make it ready for new planting. Never use sharp or pointed instruments to loosen soil because you will inevitably make deep scratches in the acrylic.

To repot the plant, add the gravel bed and the false drain-board. Now put in a layer of pea gravel with some charcoal chips. Insert a mound of soil and center the plant so that its crown is 2 inches below the top of the planter. Fill in and around with soil. Tap the container on a carpeted surface to settle the soil; add more soil around the plant, and pat it down with your fingers until the plant is securely in place. Be sure the soil is pushed down so all air pockets are eliminated.

70

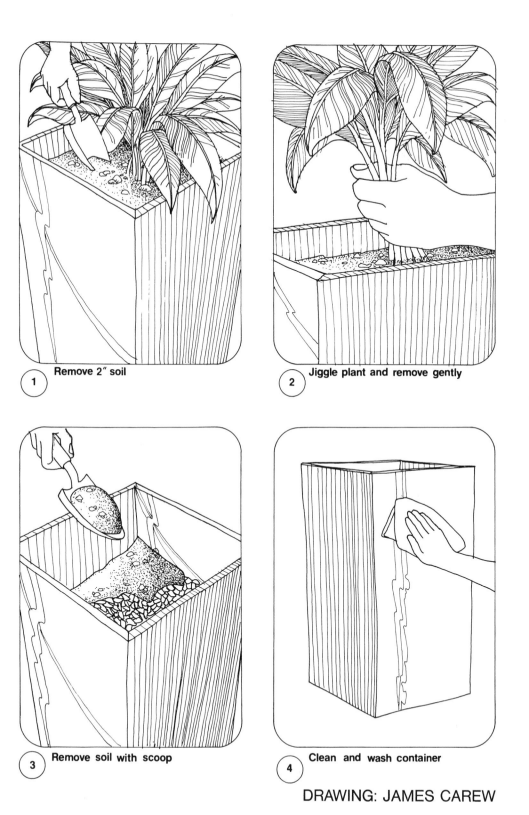

1. Remove 2″ soil

2. Jiggle plant and remove gently

3. Remove soil with scoop

4. Clean and wash container

DRAWING: JAMES CAREW

Repotting Pedestal Container

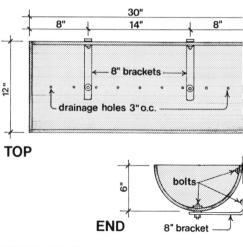

TOP

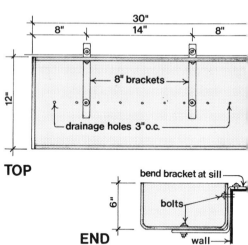

END   8" bracket

MATERIALS

SIDES: HALF A 1' DIA. X ⅜" ACRYLIC TUBE
ENDS: 1' DIA. X ⅜" DISC CUT IN HALF
SUPPORTS: 8" METAL ANGLE BRACKETS
ATTACH PLANTER W/BOLTS

TOP

bend bracket at sill

bolts

END   wall

MATERIALS

SIDES & BOTTOM: 24" X 30" X ⅜" ACRYLIC, BENT W/HE
                STRIP INTO BOX FORM
ENDS: 12" SQUARE x ⅜" ACRYLIC PIECE, CUT IN HALF
SUPPORTS: 8" METAL ANGLE BRACKETS
ATTACH PLANTER W/BOLTS

Window Boxes

DRAWING: ADRIAN MARTINE

Window Boxes

We generally think of the popular window box as a wooden product. However, it can be made of acrylic, and if used outdoors, it will withstand weather conditions as well as wood. The basic construction is simple: four sides and a bottom, with holes drilled on one parallel surface to attach it to the house wall, and four drainage holes at the bottom. If you put plants directly into the soil in the box, you might want to make it of colored acrylic to hide roots and soil. Or you can merely set potted plants in the box and fill in and around with moss.

A variation of the window box is one that has, added to the basic construction, a top with round holes cut in it to hold potted plants. This way the plants are set into the holes, providing a charming, decorative effect.

If the window is wide, use two small boxes rather than one long large box. Often large boxes are difficult to anchor to house walls, but smaller ones pose no problems. An ideal box size is 14 by 10 by 30 inches. Actually, the space will dictate the size of the window garden, but by using acrylics you can make any size necessary to fit the window.

Wall Units

Often it is desirable for decorative purposes to have plants in wall containers. There are few handsome commercial containers of this type. Do not let that stop you. A wall container is easy to make with acrylic. Use a base plate against the wall as an anchor for a cubical or cylindrical container. Bolt or screw the container to the base plate. The main thing to remember with wall containers is that they must not be too large or they will appear out of scale with the room. Keep containers small to medium, say 10 to 14 inches.

6·Plants on Display

Plant stands, pedestals, and plant platforms can make any ordinary plant extraordinary. A plant stand accommodates *many* plants in a limited space, and it can be an acrylic stepladder or a special stand with a center rod and movable disk. Pedestals are elegant and hold *one* plant; a pedestal can be 30 to 36 inches high, and of any width you desire. Plant platforms, generally 2 to 10 inches high, are used to elevate a single plant and avoid floor stains. They are functional in any area where you want to protect floors. Furthermore, all these units allow the air to reach the bottoms of pots from underneath, which discourages insects. (Gravel can be placed inside the platform bin to help furnish humidity for plants.)

With acrylic plant shelves you can grow more plants in a limited window space and have delightful, airy room accents. And under artificial light handmade units are perfect for apartment dwellers and home owners who may have to grow plants where light is limited.

Plant Stands and Ladders

Plant stands may be low or high, small or large. Manufacturers have sorely neglected plant stands; attractive commercially made

MATERIALS

DISKS: 4 at 6" DIA. x 1/4" ACRYLIC SHEET, COUNTER-
SUNK 1/4" CENTER HOLE

SUPPORTS: 4 at 1 1/2" x 2" x 9" CAST ACRYLIC BARS
W/ 1 1/2" DIA. ROUNDED ENDS, 1/4" HOLE AT
ONE END, 3/4" HOLE AT THE OTHER END

CONNECT DISK TO SUPPORT W/A 1/4" x 2 1/2" FLAT HEAD
BOLT, USE ACORN NUTS & RUBBER WASHERS

support

VERTICAL SPACERS: 6 at 1 1/2" DIA. x 6"
CAST ACRYLIC RODS W 3/4"
DIA. HOLES DRILLED THROUGH
FOR TIE ROD

TIE ROD: 3/4" DIA. x 44" CHROME ROD
THREADED AT EACH END, USE REG. &
ACORN NUTS & LOCK WASHERS

BASE: 3 - 1/2" THICK PLYWOOD DISKS; 6"DIA. W 1 1/2"
HOLE, 15"DIA. W 3/4" HOLE & 15"DIA. W 1 1/2"
HOLE, LAMINATED TOGETHER & PAINTED

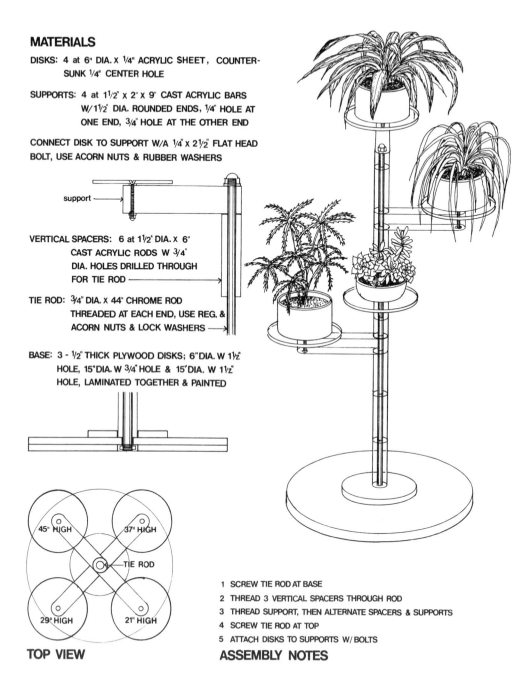

45" HIGH   37" HIGH

TIE ROD

29" HIGH   21" HIGH

TOP VIEW

1   SCREW TIE ROD AT BASE
2   THREAD 3 VERTICAL SPACERS THROUGH ROD
3   THREAD SUPPORT, THEN ALTERNATE SPACERS & SUPPORTS
4   SCREW TIE ROD AT TOP
5   ATTACH DISKS TO SUPPORTS W/ BOLTS

ASSEMBLY NOTES

Tiered Plant Stand

DRAWING: ADRIAN MARTINEZ

stands either for a group or for single-plant display are hard to find.

The stand must be carefully designed. Too large a unit can ruin the effect of a room, and too small a unit will seem insignificant and out of scale. For best results, put plant stands in room corners rather than against straight walls.

The center support for a plant stand may be either a solid acrylic or an iron rod, as long at it is stable, so the stand does not overturn easily. The design may vary, but essentially the stand has a central post and adjustable arms. Stands can hold as many as twenty plants; they are real space savers.

When you make the stand, position the disks or holders so they are not directly above each other; water dripping on plants can harm them. A good height for a plant stand is 60 inches. Make disk holders at least 8 inches in diameter, so medium as well as small plants can be displayed.

You can also make a plant stand from three acrylic 8-inch tubes, fastened to each other with acrylic bars. Potted plants can then be fitted into the tubes with the lip of the pot resting on the edge of the tube. (See drawing page 78.)

A charming small plant stand can be made in a ladder design. This unit holds many plants in a small area and looks handsome. Furthermore, it can easily be moved to decorate any room. The ladder design is shelving on an A-shaped frame, and although it is not as simple to build as some projects in this book, it certainly can be done. Use ¼-inch-thick acrylic for best results.

This Plexiglas ladder makes an excellent plant stand that is attractive and easy to clean. (Photo courtesy Rohm and Haas Co.)

MATERIALS

TUBES: 1/4" THICK ACRYLIC
DIAMETER SHOULD ALLOW FOR
POT LIP TO SIT ON ITS EDGE,
VARY HEIGHTS

(OPTIONAL)
BRACES: 3 at 3/4" x 2" x 4" SOLID
ACRYLIC BARS, ATTACHED
TO TUBES W/ METAL TAPPING
SCREWS IN PRE DRILLED HOLES

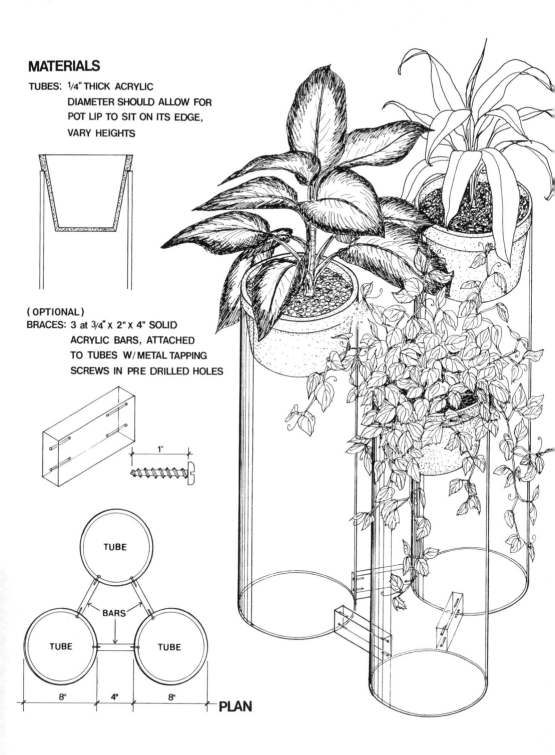

1"

TUBE

BARS

TUBE   TUBE

8"   4"   8"

PLAN

Tubular Plant Stand

DRAWING: ADRIAN MARTINEZ

A platform or pedestal elevates a plant and makes it more attractive than if set on a table or desk. (Photo by author)

Pedestals

Furniture pedestals for potted plants are invariably expensive. There are some lovely ones available, but you might want to make your own to suit the decor of the room and to save money. A pedestal can be tall and narrow or low and wide, depending upon the size of the pot and the scale of the room furnishings. Use a tall pedestal as a vertical accent. A squat pedestal is ideal for a very large plant—you need mass to balance weight so that the pedestal and plant complement each other.

An assortment of easy-to-make plant pedestals. (Photo by author)

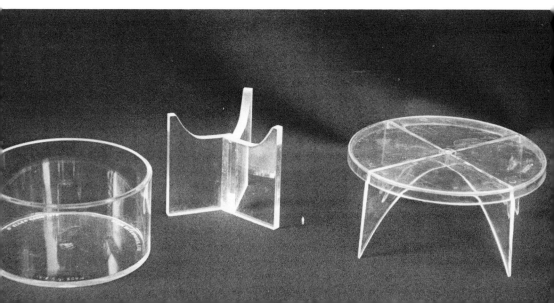

A small planter like this may be filled with gravel and a potted plant placed on top. (Photo by author)

Cylindrical acrylic pedestals can be handsome too. When fitted with a disk top they are perfect for a plant or vase. You can also group three pedestals of varying height to create a mass planting—an effective way to decorate a corner. With pedestals you will need saucers to catch drainage water; use the acrylic ones now available in most nurseries.

Platforms

Because more and more people are using large potted plants as indoor decoration, the floor plant stand or tray has become a necessity. Yet, at this writing, I have not seen one commercially manufactured plant platform. Platforms elevate a plant so you can see it to better advantage. The plant always looks better, since plant and platform become a harmonious whole. And, of course, the plant platform eliminates stains on wood surfaces.

Ideally, platforms are 2 to 6 inches deep and 8 to 10 inches wide by 10 to 14 inches in length. You can easily construct them from acrylic in a bin style. Use redwood slats spaced 1 inch apart on top of the bin, or set plants directly on a gravel bed in the bin.

ATERIALS

LL STRUTS: 6 at ¾" X 1½" X 12", REDWOOD

LL SPACERS: 2 at ¾" X 1½" X 16½", REDWOOD

ACH W/FINISHING NAILS & GLUE

AY SIDES: 2 each at 2" X 18" & 2" X 11½", BUTT JOINTS

AY BASE: 1 at 11½" X 17½", CEMENTED TO SIDES

¼" ACRYLIC PLASTIC

STRUTS

SPACER

lant Tray

DRAWING: ADRIAN MARTINEZ

Shelves

Shelving for plants can have many advantages in a window. You can grow many plants in a small area, and the window greenery is attractive and adds drama to a room. The usual acrylic shelf can be used (three lengths to a window perhaps), but a more unusual and interesting design is to use triangular or disk shapes. These shelves can accommodate large pots, whereas the narrow window shelf we are so accustomed to seeing has limitations.

The ideal straight shelving should be 8 inches wide and never longer than 36 inches. Center supports will be needed. Triangles of 10 by 10 by 10 inches are fine for accommodating larger pots, and 10-inch disks are perfect for most house plant containers.

Artificial Light Units

There are commercial units available for growing plants under lights, but many of them are rather institutional in appearance and few blend with contemporary interiors. If you want to grow plants under artificial light, you should make your own unit so the garden can become part of the room and otherwise barren areas can be used for greenery.

A shelf unit of acrylic is shown in drawing opposite. This box-type design is simple yet pleasing and it fits into almost any room decor; use large plants. The acrylic may be clear, colored or mirrored to match interiors. Other units, too, can be constructed from acrylic and wood and can decorate desks and tables or shelves; use small plants with these.

Scale and proportion, as well as the kinds of plants you will grow, are very important when you design your artificial-light unit. Some plants, such as angel-wing begonias, are very tall, so ample height will be needed for displaying them. Other plants are sprawling, so a wide unit is necessary. Whichever unit you use, try to make the shelves adjustable so that as plants grow

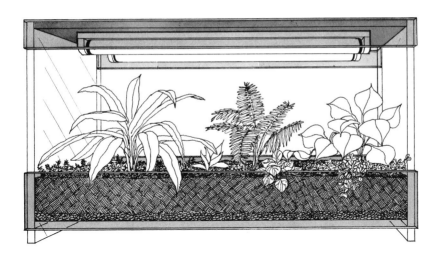

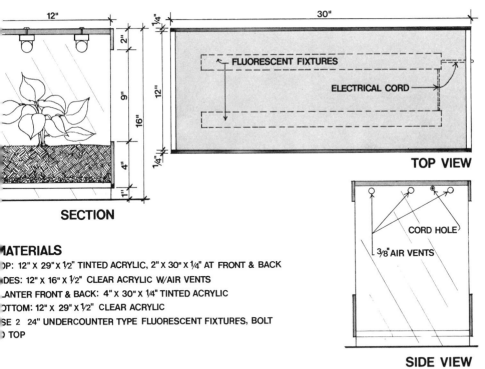

12"

30"

FLUORESCENT FIXTURES

ELECTRICAL CORD

1/4"

2"

9"

12"

16"

4"

1/4"

1"

TOP VIEW

SECTION

CORD HOLE

3/8" AIR VENTS

MATERIALS

OP: 12" X 29" X 1/2" TINTED ACRYLIC, 2" X 30" X 1/4" AT FRONT & BACK

DES: 12" X 16" X 1/2" CLEAR ACRYLIC W/AIR VENTS

LANTER FRONT & BACK: 4" X 30" X 1/4" TINTED ACRYLIC

OTTOM: 12" X 29" X 1/2" CLEAR ACRYLIC

SE 2 24" UNDERCOUNTER TYPE FLUORESCENT FIXTURES, BOLT

) TOP

SIDE VIEW

Acrylic Light Unit

DRAWING: ADRIAN MARTINEZ

they can be moved away from the light and still be accommodated within the unit.

The bookcase- or divider-type artificial-light unit is popular because besides looking handsome it serves a purpose. This garden under lights becomes an adjunct to the room and as such must be designed to harmonize with its other furnishings. Acrylic plastics seem to fit into any decor, so this material can be used to great advantage. Furthermore, the clear quality of acrylics is simple and elegant, and acrylic never gets dirty or decayed as some woods do. (For plants for all of these units see Chapter 7.)

When designing the light garden, also keep in mind that plants under lights keep growing all the time and must have enough humidity, air circulation and moisture. There are many fine books on the subject of growing plants under artificial light that will help you as you go along. You may want to refer to these:

Fluorescent Light Gardening, Elaine Cherry, Van Nostrand, 1965

The Indoor Light Gardening Book, George Elbert, Crown Publishers, 1973,

Plants Under Lights, Jack Kramer, Simon and Schuster, 1974.

7·Plant Lists

Plants for Terrariums

Small plants or true miniatures make the best terrarium subjects. They grow slowly and stay small for many months in enclosed cases. Plants that prefer high humidity and a bright but not sunny location are prime candidates too. You can buy terrarium plants from local nurseries or from mail-order houses. Here are some good plants for your terrariums:

Acorus gramineus pusillus (sweet flag)
Tuftlike grassy leaves; 2 to 3 inches high. Excellent terrarium plant.

Aglaonema commutatum (Chinese evergreen)
Dark green leaves with silver markings; slow-growing.

Allophyton mexicanum
Only 4 inches high. Dark green leaves; lavender and white flowers. Almost everblooming.

Asplenium platyneuron (ebony spleenwort)
Feathery fronds and brown-purple stems. Large but good.

Begonia boweri
Old-time favorite, with bright green foliage and black stitched leaves.

B. dregei
Gnarled-type growth. Bronze-red, maple-shaped leaves. Always good.

B. rotundifolia
Apple-green foliage; handsome.

Calathea bachemiana
Not really a miniature, but a lush plant with velvety gray-green leaves edged with dark green. Also handsome is *C. picturata argentea,* with silver leaves etched in dark green.

Camptosorus rhizophyllus (walking fern)
One of the best tiny ferns, with wedge-shaped leaves.

Chlorophytum bichetii
Rosettes of lovely green, grassy leaves with white stripes.

Crassula cooperi
Three-inch leathery-leaved plant.

C. schmidtii
A handsome plant, with red-tinted leaves. Many other small species available. Use only in open terrariums.

Acorus gramineus, *with grassy leaves, adds a graceful touch to terrariums; it does well in a closed case. (Photo courtesy Merry Gardens)*

Asplenium is a leafy fern that provides excellent color in small gardens. (Photo courtesy Merry Gardens)

Cryptanthus bromelioides tricolor
One of the best small bromeliads, with rosettes of green leaves striped pink and white. *C. bivattatus* (*Roseus picta*) bears bronze-pink foliage striped pale green, *C. acaulis* (star plant) and *C. terminalis* have bronze-green foliage, and *C. beuckeri* has pale green foliage.

Davallia bullata (mariesis) (rabbit's foot fern)
Creeping brown rhizomes, lacy fronds. Select small plants; can grow large.

Dracaena sanderiana
Deep green leaves lined white; rosette growth. Needs space.

D. warneckii
Rosette-type plant with spear-shaped dark green leaves finely marked with white. Very handsome.

Ficus pumila (repens)
Heart-shaped dark green foliage; sends out disks that cling to sides of terrarium.

Full of color and with a black-stitched leaf is Begonia boweri *'Chantilly Lace'. (Photo by Joyce R. Wilson)*

Fittonia verschaffeltii (mosaic plant)
   A creeper, with iridescent foliage; grows slowly and remains dwarf size. Excellent.

Haworthia fasciata (zebra haworthia)
   A small plant, with dark green leaves banded crosswise with rows of white dots.

Humata tyermannii (bear's-foot fern)
   Small and delicate; very lacy fronds. Excellent.

Kleinia repens (blue chalk sticks)
   Looks like its common name: blue-green cylindrical leaves in clusters.

Malpighia coccigera (miniature holly)
   Glossy green leaves and pink flowers. Robust.

Maranta leuconeura kerchoveana (prayer plant)
   Low-growing plant with beautiful tapestry-like leaves. Spectacular. Also try *M. massangeana*, with satiny bluish-green leaves reticulated with silver.

Microlepia setosa
   Tiny delicate fern with feathery fronds. Good.

Pellaea rotundifolia (button fern)
Tiny button leaves of dark green on wiry stems. Choice terrarium plant.

Pellionia repens
Creeper, with elliptical metal-green foliage; stays small.

Peperomias
Another group of excellent terrarium subjects, with decorative foliage. Leaf colors vary from greens to browns to maroon and variegated. Generally plants stay low and bushy.

  Peperomia bicolor
  Handsome olive-gray velvety leaves beautifully ribbed with silver.

  P. caperata 'Emerald Queen'
  Heart-shaped emerald-green leaves. Choice.

  P. fosteriana
  Rounded, dark green leaves. Lighter veins. Slow-growing; good.

  P. griseo argentea
  Quilted and thin silvery leaves with purple-olive veining. Grows in low rosette.

Haworthias are fine small plants for desert-type terrariums; H. fasciata on the right is a favorite. (Photo by Joyce R. Wilson)

Peperomias are favorites in the terrarium. Left to right: P. cluisiaefolia, P. rubella *and* P. crassiflora. (*Photo courtesy Merry Gardens*)

P. sandersii (watermelon peperomia)
Silver-and-green-striped leaf.

Pilea
A vast group of fine terrarium plants, generally bushy, and of the easiest culture. Leaf coloring varies from dark green to brownish green and to silver markings. Plants need a bright location (no sun) and average humidity to do their best. Trim occasionally to keep attractive.

Pilea cadierei minima (aluminum plant)
Lovely and tiny silvery leaves.

P. nummulariaefolia (creeping Charlie)
Light green foliage on trailing stems.

P. serpyllacea
A somewhat larger-growing Pilea.

Polystichum tsus-simense
An old favorite. Tiny feathery fern with great charm.

Pteris cretica 'Wilsonii' (table or brake fern)
Low and bushy, crested fern; stays small. Excellent. Many varieties.

Punica granatum nana (dwarf pomegranate)
Lovely little-leaved tree with red flowers. Prune and shape as desired.
P. 'Chico' is good too.

Rosa (rose)
These diminutive replicas of their larger cousins are always desirable, and in some gardens they are elegant. Plants rarely grow more than 14 inches. Try these miniature roses for a stellar sight:

'Bo-Peep'
Lovely double pink flowers; prolific bloomer.

'Cinderella'
Old standby, with full, pink flowers; likes coolness (60° F.).

'Lilac Time'
Only 8 inches tall; bears splendid lilac flowers.

Miniature roses make a fine color display in terrariums; there are dozens of varieties available. (Photo courtesy Wayside Gardens)

'Lollipop'
Fine variety, with beautiful fiery red flowers.

'Midget'
Tiny and fragrant; deep rose flowers.

'Pink Heather'
Blooms abundantly, with double pink flowers.

'Pixie'
Well known and adored; tiny white flowers. Very small.

'Red Imp'
Intense red flowers make this one outstanding.

Saintpaulia (African violet)

These have been favorites for years, and the miniatures make any terrarium glow with color. Some plants bloom on and off through the year, with lavender, rose, or purple blooms. Plants will need some ventilation, so remove terrarium cover for a few hours a week.

Saintpaulia 'Honeyette'
Double red-lavender flowers. Only 5 inches.

S. 'Lavender Elfin Girl'
Ruffled and fluted foliage; lavender flowers.

S. 'Pink Rock'
Quilted leaves and single pink blooms.

S. 'Sweet Sixteen'
Double white flowers, scalloped spoon-shaped leaves.

S. 'Tinkle'
Fluted and ruffled foliage. Lavender blooms.

S. 'Tiny Bells'
Quilted dark green leaves; blue flowers.

S. 'Wendy'
Quilted leaves; large blue blooms.

S. 'White Doll'
Only 2 inches high, with white flowers.

Saxifraga sarmentosa (strawberry geranium)

One of the best terrarium plants. A few inches high and slow growing. Excellent for gardens. Blackish-green lobed leaves.

Scindapsus aureus (ivy-arum)
   Handsome heart-shaped leaves; keep pruned.

Sinningia pusilla
   One of the finest miniatures. To 1 inch, with stellar pink blooms. Not to be missed. Three varieties are available: 'Wood Nymph', 'Dollbaby' and 'Priscilla'.

Plants for Hanging Gardens

For basket growing, select plants that have a natural trailing habit or those with rosette-type growth, e.g., many ferns. To be truly handsome, the basket plant should be lush and full. Try some of the following in your handcrafted acrylic containers:

Abutilon hybridum (flowering maple)
   Hollyhock-type flowers in many colors. These plants have maple-shaped leaves and colorful blossoms through spring and summer.

Achimenes (rainbow flower)
   This colorful plant has small leaves and bright flowers.

A popular terrarium plant is Saxifragra sarmentosa, *called strawberry geranium. (Photo courtesy Merry Gardens)*

For a splash of color use campanulas in hanging baskets. (Photo courtesy Merry Gardens)

Begonia foliosa *is a favorite small pendant plant that looks well in hanging containers. (Photo by Joyce R. Wilson)*

Cissus, commonly known as grape ivy, makes a fine hanging plant and grows readily even in dim light. (Photo by Joyce R. Wilson)

Asparagus

Two kinds of asparagus plants have been favorites for a long time but only recently have become appreciated as hanging-basket plants. *A. plumosus* is a true climber; *A. sprengeri* (the emerald fern) has arching fronds of feathery green. Either one is a stalwart performer in a basket.

Begonia foliosa

Tiny-leaved plant; dark green and bushy.

Beloperone guttata (shrimp plant)

The shrimp plant has coral-colored bracts and deep green leaves. A bushy plant.

Bougainvillea (paper flower)

A lovely, popular vine that is exquisite in summer, with bright red or orange bracts and dark green leaves. The orange variety is somewhat difficult to grow, so ask for *Bougainvillea* 'Barbara Karst' or *B.* 'San Diego Red'.

Campanula

Campanula comes from the bellflower family. It has handsome colorful flowers—blue or white—that make it a desirable basket subject. There are several varieties that have single or double flowers in white, light blue or intense blue. The most popular campanulas are *C. fragilis* (purplish blue) and *C. isophylla* (light blue). Campanulas are small- to medium-sized plants and never grow to large proportions, so they are ideal for a limited space.

Chlorophytum elatum (spider plant)

These grow as easily as weeds, and with their graceful, grassy leaves and hanging plantlets they make a lovely display within a year.

Cissus

These relatives of the grape family are excellent indoors where tough plants are needed. The best one is *C. rhombifolia* (grape ivy), which has glossy, toothed, and pointed leaves. It will climb if you furnish support (string will do), or it will cascade over the pot rim. *C. antarctica* (the kangaroo vine), another fine species for baskets, has long and narrow, brown-veined, dark green, toothed leaves; needs little care.

Clerodendrum thomsoniae (glory-bower)

There are many fine clerodendrums, but this is the best one for baskets. It has beautiful crimson flowers, with pure white calyx and lovely green leaves.

Davallia fejeensis (rabbit's-foot fern)

Graceful fern, with fragile apple-green fronds.

Dipladenia amoena (Mexican love vine)

Also sold under the name Mandevilla, this is a real stunner. Similar to a morning glory, it offers a bounty of bright rose-pink flowers.

Ficus pumila (or repens) (creeping fig)

This fine creeping plant with tiny 1-inch leaves is never spectacular but always desirable. Grows into a dense ball of color if given plenty of water and a well-ventilated location.

Gynura sarmentosa (velvet plant)

With purple leaves, this plant glows with color in good light. It adapts well to basket growing and becomes a lush display.

Hedera helix (English ivy)

Scores of superb ivies with exquisite foliage are at nurseries. Some have dark green leaves; others are variegated. Because of their airy quality they are handsome plants, but they do have some stringent requirements. Most need coolness (about 58° F. at night) and are subject to attack by spider mites.

Hoya carnosa (wax plant)

Waxlike flowers and gray-green oval leaves.

Plectranthus is the popular Swedish ivy, and this is the small-leaved variegated form. (Photo by author)

Impatiens

These are rarely considered basket plants, but they certainly are at their best in a hanging garden. Select the small-leaved variety called 'Elfin'. It is floriferous, and a well-grown plant will be a cloud of color.

Lantana montevidensis

In a hanging container lantana is a beautiful display, with its cascading green foliage and superb clusters of lavender flowers.

Myrsine nummularia

This is a miniature plant, with buttonlike, glossy green leaves on wiry stems. It never grows too large and is ideal where a small spot of color is needed.

Petunias

Everyone is familiar with these grand flowers, and the cascading varieties are stunning in bloom in midsummer; pots overflow with blossoms. Many colors are available, but to me the deep red varieties are the prettiest.

Plectranthus coleoides (Swedish ivy)

Rounded and scalloped bright green leaves. Bushy and pendant.

Rhoeo discolor (Moses-in-the-cradle)

Not really a trailer but a handsome, easy-to-grow plant from Mexico and the West Indies, with stiff rosettes of dark green, almost black, leaves that are purple underneath.

Saxifraga sarmentosa (strawberry geranium)

Soft, round, hairy leaves that are purple underneath. Popular.

Zebrina pendula *is bushy and bright and used frequently as a hanging plant. (Photo by author)*

Scindapsus aureus

This fine plant and its many varieties make stellar basket gardens. The original species *S. aureus* has heart-shaped dark green leaves marbled with yellow. Many varieties have smaller leaves, some with pure white markings.

Sedum morganianum (burro's tail)

Unusual plant, with beadlike gray-green leaves on long pendant stems.

S. sieboldii

Small and round gray-green leaves; pendant growth.

Senecio rowleyanus (green-pea plant)

Aptly fits its common name: strings of green-pealike leaves.

Syngonium (sometimes called Nephthytis)

Syngoniums have decorative leaf shapes, ranging from a simple arrowhead design to unequal-sized segments. Foliage leaf color is out-

A variegated form of tradescantia, this leafy plant looks handsome in a basket. (Photo by author)

standing: many are colorfully variegated with yellow, chartreuse, white, or silver markings.

Tolmiea menziesii (piggyback plant)
   This is a curious plant with thin, light green leaves; new plantlets grow at the bases of the mature leaves.

Tradescantia fluminensis (wandering Jew)
   Similar to Zebrina and often confused with it, some of these plants have large blue-green leaves; others have green-and-white foliage. *T. fluminensis* is the species most often seen, but *T. blossfeldiana,* with reddish-purple leaves, is more suitable for hanging baskets.

Zebrina pendula (wandering Jew)
   With thickened trailing stems and glistening foliage striped with silver, pink or white, Zebrina has long oval leaves that grow rapidly, and plants soon fill a basket.

Plants for Pedestals

Any plant can be placed on a pedestal to elevate it, but larger specimens (those in pots over 10 inches) are best—smaller plants appear out of scale and look better on plant stands or on window shelves. Plants with rosette-type growth or a cascading habit are generally the best types to use.

Agave americana marginata (century plant)
Can grow very large; green leaves, edged in yellow. Rosette growth.

Aglaonema commutatum (Chinese evergreen)
Grows to 3 feet; silver markings on dark green leaves.

Ananas comosus (pineapple plant)
A 30- to 36-inch rosette of spiny, dark green leaves.

Begonia *'Maphil' is also known as* Begonia *'Cleopatra'. Either way, it is a handsome plant.* (*Photo by author*)

There are many aglaonemas, and these are leafy pretty plants for pedestal growing. (*Photo courtesy Merry Gardens*)

Asparagus sprengeri (emerald fern)
Feathery emerald-green fronds.

Asplenium nidus (bird's-nest fern)
Broad, wavy, apple-green fronds.

Begonia crestabruchi (lettuce-leaf begonia)
Heavily ruffled yellow-green leaves.

B. 'Maphil'
Resembles a castor-bean plant, with large leaves, multicolored.

Caladiums
Popular, with lance-shaped leaves; many varieties in an array of color.

Chlorophytum elatum
Glossy, green, graceful foliage; rosette growth.

Cissus rhombifolia (grape ivy)
Dark green scalloped leaves.

101

Echeverias are easy to grow and make fine easy-to-care-for house plants. (Photo courtesy Merry Gardens)

A very handsome plant is Hoffmannia refulgens, *and it can grow quite large. (Photo courtesy Merry Gardens)*

Davallia fejeensis plumosa
Dainty frilly plant, with feathery fronds. Sprawling.

Echeveria
Succulent, with beautiful leaf rosettes. Many species available.

Gardenia jasminoides
Lush, bushy plant, with shiny green leaves.

Guzmania monostachia
A rosette of lush green leaves.

Hibiscus rosa-sinensis
Big sprawling plant, with fresh green leaves and large flowers.

Hoffmannia refulgens
Crinkled leaves; bushy and lush.

Ligularia kaempferi argentea (leopard plant)
Green leaves with creamy white margins.

Neoregelias have handsome rosette growth and make pretty plants on tables or pedestals. (Photo by author)

Philodendron *'Burgundy'* brings deep rich color into the home and is an easy plant to grow. (*Photo courtesy Merry Gardens*)

With lovely rosette growth, Pandanus veitchii *is a fine pedestal plant for a living-room accent.* (*Photo by author*)

Leafy and bushy is Philodendron panduraeforme, *which can grow quite tall and is suitable for a pedestal. (Photo courtesy Merry Gardens)*

Medinilla magnifica
Large, dark green foliage plant.

Monstera deliciosa (Swiss-cheese plant)
Big cutleaf beauty.

Neoregelia carolinae
Dark green, straplike leaves; rosette.

Nephrolepis (Boston fern)
Many fine varieties. Rosettes.

Pandanus veitchii (screw pine)
Variegated graceful leaves; rosette.

Philodendron
Large group of several good species. Select large-leaved ones.

Plectranthus coleoides (Swedish ivy)
Crinkled and scalloped bright green leaves.

Polypodium aureum glaucum (hare's-foot fern)
Large blue-gray fronds. Pendant.

Always a favorite is Rhapis excelsa, *an amenable plant that looks good anywhere.*

Raphis excelsa (lady palm)
  Low bushy palm, with glossy green leaves.

Schizocentron elegans (Spanish shawl)
  Creeping plant, with hairy dark green leaves and purple blooms.

Smithiantha zebrina
  Rounded dark green leaves; large and bushy.

Vriesia hieroglyphica
  Green-banded rosette. Handsome.

Woodwardia orientalis (chain fern)
  Big, sprawling, dark green fern.

Plants for Artificial Light Units

Almost any house plant will prosper when grown under artificial light. Just what you grow depends on how much light you are using. For two-tube fluorescent lamps, select low-light-level foliage plants such as aspidistras, aglaonemas, philodendrons and cissus species. Flowering plants will require more light (a four-lamp unit, perhaps). Any of the terrarium or hanging plants and some of the smaller pedestal plants already described can be grown under lights.

Acrylic Dealers

ALABAMA

PPG Industries, Inc.
915 N. 18th St.
Birmingham (35201)

PPG Industries, Inc.
610 Seminary St.
Florence (35630)

PPG Industries, Inc.
310 S. Royal St .
Mobile (36602)

PPG Industries, Inc.
2004 Eighth St.
Tuscaloosa (35401)

ARIZONA

Antex Plastics, Inc.
808 N. 17th Ave.
Phoenix (85007)

Cadillac Plastic & Chemical Co.
1152 E. Indian School Rd.
Phoenix (85014)

PPG Industries, Inc.
1140 N. 21st Ave.
Phoenix (85005)

ARKANSAS

PPG Industries, Inc.
1500 E. Washington Ave.
Little Rock (72114)

CALIFORNIA

Cadillac Plastic & Chemical Co.
Division Dayco Corporation
1531 S. State College Rd.
Anaheim (92802)

Corth Plastics
725 Delaware St.
Berkeley (95071)

CALIFORNIA (*cont.*)

Los Angeles Metropolitan Area:
Cadillac Plastic & Chemical Co.
Division Dayco Corporation
2305 W. Beverly Blvd.
Los Angeles (90057)

Gem O'Lite Plastics Corporation
5525 Cahuenga Blvd.
North Hollywood (91601)

Plastic Center, Inc., of Los
  Angeles
186 S. Alvarado
Los Angeles (90057)

Port Plastics, Inc.
8037 E. Slauson Ave.
Montebello (90640)

Tyre Brothers
3008 S. San Pedro
Los Angeles (90011)

Terrell's Plastics
3618 Broadway
Sacramento (95817)

Ridout Plastics Company
1875 Hancock St.
San Diego (92110)

San Francisco Metropolitan Area:
Cadillac Plastic & Chemical
  Company
Division Dayco Corporation
313 Corey Way
South San Francisco (94080)

Cobbledick-Kibbe Glass Co.
301 Washington St.
Oakland (94607)

Corth Plastics
532 Howland Ave.
Redwood City (94063)

Plastic Sales, Inc.
863 Folsom Blvd.
San Francisco (94107)

Port Plastics, Inc.
180 Constitution Dr.
Menlo Park (94025)

Transilwrap West Corporation
274 Harbor Way
San Francisco (94080)

COLORADO

PPG Industries, Inc.
3120 N. El Paso St.
P.O. Box 3283
North End Station
Colorado Springs (80907)

Regal Plastic Supply Company
407 Auburn Dr.
Colorado Springs (80909)

Plasticrafts, Inc.
2800 Speer Blvd. N.
Denver (80211)

PPG Industries, Inc.
590 Quivas St.
P.O. Box 1978
Denver (80201)

PPG Industries, Inc.
210 N. Greenwood
P.O. Box 4098
Pueblo (81003)

CONNECTICUT

Modern Plastics & Glass, Inc.
678 Howard Ave.
Bridgeport (06605)

Hartford Metropolitan Area:
Cadillac Plastic & Chemical Co.
Division Dayco Corporation
823–827 Windsor St.
Hartford (06120)

Commercial Plastics & Supply
100 Prestige Park Rd.
East Hartford (06108)

Industrial Plastic Supply Division
Industrial Safety Supply Co., Inc.
547 New Park Ave.
West Hartford (06107)

PPG Industries, Inc.
400 Windsor St.
West Hartford (06120)

PPG Industries, Inc.
100 Woodmont Rd.
Milford (06460)

Commercial Plastics & Supply
  Corporation
463 Boston Post Rd.
Orange (06477)

Modern Plastics & Glass, Inc.
1244 E. Main St.
Stamford (06922)

DELAWARE

Franklin Fibre-Lamitex
  Corporation
903 E. 13th St.
Wilmington (19802)

Kaufman Glass Company
1209–21 French St.
Wilmington (19899)

PPG Industries, Inc.
1920 Hutton St.
Wilmington (19802)

DISTRICT OF COLUMBIA

Commercial Plastics & Supply
  Corporation
5217 Monroe Pl.
Hyattsville (20781)

Glass Distributors, Inc.
Plastic Division
1741 Johnson Ave. N.W.
Washington (20009)

PPG Industries, Inc.
4601 Emerson St.
Hyattsville (20781)

Read Plastics
12331 Wilkins Ave.
Rockville (20852)

PPG Industries, Inc.
400 E. Main St.
Salisbury (21801)

FLORIDA

Commercial Plastics & Supply
  Corporation
2331 N. Laura St.
Jacksonville (32206)

PPG Industries, Inc.
601 N. Myrtle Ave.
P.O. Box 2240
Jacksonville (32203)

Miami Metropolitan Area:
Commercial Plastics & Supply
  Corporation
3801 N.W. Second Ave.
Miami (33137)

Faulkner, Inc.
1855 W. Okeechobee Rd.
Hialeah (33010)

Modern Plastics
7175 W. 20th Ave.
Hialeah (33012)

PPG Industries, Inc.
17851 N.W. Miami Ct.
P.O. Box 3680, Norland Branch
Miami (33169)

Commercial Plastics & Supply
  Corporation
4096 S. Orange Ave.
Orlando (32806)

FLORIDA (cont.)

Modern Plastics
580 Fairvilla Rd.
Orlando (32808)

PPG Industries, Inc.
1705 S. Division St.
P.O. Box 152
Orlando (32805)

Modern Plastics
913 N. "P" St.
Pensacola (32505)

PPG Industries, Inc.
3820 Liggett St.
P.O. Box 27
Pensacola (32502)

Modern Plastics
2850 47th Ave. N.
St. Petersburg (33714)

PPG Industries, Inc.
2222 First Ave.
P.O. Box 10369
St. Petersburg (33733)

Faulkner Plastics, Inc.
1091 Central Ave.
Sarasota (33580)

PPG Industries, Inc.
326 W. Georgia St.
Tallahassee (32302)

Faulkner Plastics, Inc.
4504 E. Hillsboro Ave.
Tampa (33601)

PPG Industries, Inc.
137 S. Tampa St.
P.O. Box 1169
Tampa (33601)

PPG Industries, Inc.
2526 Okeechobee Rd.
P.O. Box 2666
West Palm Beach (33402)

GEORGIA

PPG Industries, Inc.
237 Flint Ave.
Albany (31701)

Atlanta Metropolitan Area:
A.A.A. Brands
515 Means St. N.W.
Atlanta (30318)

Cadillac Plastic & Chemical
  Company
Division Dayco Corporation
1500 Carroll Dr. N.W.
Atlanta (30318)

Commercial Plastics & Supply
  Corporation
554 North Ave. N.W.
Atlanta (30318)

PPG Industries, Inc.
824 Memorial Dr. S.E.
P.O. Box 1458
Atlanta (30316)

Transilwrap Co. of Atlanta, Inc.
3616 McCall Pl.
Doraville (30040)

PPG Industries, Inc.
1230 Reynolds St.
Augusta (30903)

PPG Industries, Inc.
818 Riverside Dr.
P.O. Box 1464
Macon (31202)

PPG Industries, Inc.
202 W. Third St.
P.O. Box 1484
Rome (30161)

PPG Industries, Inc.
Victory Dr. & Bull St.
P.O. Box 3397, Station A
Savannah (31413)

ILLINOIS

Chicago Metropolitan Area:
Auburn Plastic Engineering Co.
Division Plastic Warehousing
  Corporation
4916 S. Loomis Blvd.
Chicago (60609)

Cadillac Plastic & Chemical Co.
Division Dayco Corporation
1245 W. Fulton
Chicago (60606)

Colonial Kolonite Company
2232 W. Armitage Ave.
Chicago (60647)

Commercial Plastics & Supply
4334 Chicago Ave.
Chicago (60651)

Nering's Plastics Inc.
2420 Oakton St., Bldg. K
Arlington Heights (60005)

PPG Industries, Inc.
4850 S. Kilbourn Ave.
Chicago (60632)

Transilwrap Company
2615 N. Paulina St.
Chicago (60614)

PPG Industries, Inc.
234 W. Cerro Gordo St.
P.O. Box 1272
Decatur (62525)

Almac Plastics Inc.
10129 Pacific Ave.
Franklin Park (60131)

Cope Plastics, Inc.
1111 W. Delmar Ave.
Godfrey (62035)

Cope Plastics Illinois, Inc.
2341 Fifth Ave.
Moline (61265)

Cope Plastics, Inc.
8206 N. University Ave.
Peoria (61614)

PPG Industries, Inc.
8202 N. University Ave.
Peoria (61602)

PPG Industries, Inc.
1016 E. Jackson St.
P.O. Box 2270
Springfield (62703)

INDIANA

PPG Industries, Inc.
5415 Distributor Dr.
Fort Wayne (46801)

Nering's Plastics, Inc.
155 E. 61st Ave.
Merrillville
Gary (46410)

PPG Industries, Inc.
1301 W. Ridge Rd.
Gary (46408)

Cadillac Plastic & Chemical Co.
Division Dayco Corporation
825 Meridian St. S.
Indianapolis (46225)

Hyaline Plastics Corporation
P.O. Box 523
1019 Capitol Ave.
Indianapolis (46204)

PPG Industries, Inc.
59 S. State Ave.
Indianapolis (46201)

PPG Industries, Inc.
110 W. Washington St.
Muncie (47305)

PPG Industries, Inc.
1918 S. Franklin St.
South Bend (46613)

PPG Industries, Inc.
1301 Eagle St.
P.O. Box 396
Terre Haute (47807)

PPG Industries, Inc.
908 S. 15th St.
Vincennes (47591)

IOWA

Cope Plastics, Inc.
714–66th Ave. S.W.
Cedar Rapids (52404)

IOWA (*cont.*)

PPG Industries, Inc.
310 Eighth Ave. S.E.
Cedar Rapids (52406)

Cadillac Plastic & Chemical Co.
Division Dayco Corporation
North Brady Industrial Park
Davenport (52802)

PPG Industries, Inc.
147 S. Sturdevant St.
P.O. Box 3428
Davenport (52805)

PPG Industries, Inc.
700 New York Ave.
P.O. Box 1615
Des Moines (60306)

Van Horn Plastics
8000 University Ave.
Des Moines (50311)

PPG Industries, Inc.
517 Central Ave.
P.O. Box 1254
Ft. Dodge (50501)

PPG Industries, Inc.
122 Lafayette St.
Iowa City (52240)

PPG Industries, Inc.
611 Bluff St.
P.O. Box 2277
Waterloo (50705)

KANSAS

Cadillac Plastic & Chemical Co.
Division Dayco Corporation
9025 Lenexa Dr.
Lenexa (Kansas City) (66215)

PPG Industries, Inc.
1212 Kansas Ave.
P.O. Box 558
Topeka (66601)

PPG Industries, Inc.
145 Pattie St.
Wichita (67211)

Regal Plastic Supply Company
329 N. Indiana St.
Wichita (67214)

KENTUCKY

Cadillac Plastic & Chemical Co.
Division Dayco Corporation
3927 Park Dr.
Louisville (40216)

General Rubber & Supply Co.,
  Inc.
3118 S. Preston St.
Louisville (40213)

PPG Industries, Inc.
1421 Hess La.
Louisville (40217)

PPG Industries, Inc.
128 S. Third St.
Paducah (42001)

LOUISIANA

Gulf Wandes Corporation
8325 S. Choctaw Dr.
P.O. Box 15925
Baton Rouge (70815)

PPG Industries, Inc.
7755 Commerce Dr.
P.O. Box 15909
Baton Rouge (70815)

New Orleans Metropolitan Area:
Cadillac Plastic & Chemical Co.
Division Dayco Corporation
2605 Ridgelake Dr.
Metairie (70002)

Gulf Wandes Corporation
P.O. Box 15456
404 Marengo St.
New Orleans (70115)

PPG Industries, Inc.
5600 Hayne Blvd.
P.O. Box 52258
New Orleans (70150)

Zinsel Glass & Supply Company
612 Airline Hwy.
Metairie (70002)

PPG Industries, Inc.
525 Cotton St.
P.O. Box 1137
Shreveport (71112)

Regal Plastic Supply Company
828 Wilson St.
Shreveport (71101)

MARYLAND

Baltimore Metropolitan Area:
Almac Plastics of Maryland, Inc.
6311 Erdman Ave.
Baltimore (21205)

Bronze & Plastic Specialties, Inc.
2025 Inverness Ave.
Baltimore (21230)

Cadillac Plastic & Chemical Co.
Division Dayco Corporation
650 North Point Rd.
Baltimore (21206)

Commercial Plastics & Supply
   Corporation
1130 E. 30th St.
Baltimore (21218)

PPG Industries, Inc.
10820 Gilroy Rd.
Cockeysville (21030)

PPG Industries, Inc.
650 Frederick Rd.
P.O. Box 529
Hagerstown (21740)

PPG Industries, Inc.
509 National Hwy.
P.O. Box 3386
Levale (21502)

MASSACHUSETTS

Boston Metropolitan Area:
Cadillac Plastic & Chemical Co.
Division Dayco Corporation
269 McGrath Hwy.
Somerville (02143)

Commercial Plastics & Supply
   Corporation
352 McGrath Hwy.
Somerville (02143)

Insulfab Plastics, Inc.
69 Grove St.
Watertown (02172)

PPG Industries, Inc.
887 Main St.
Melrose (02176)

PPG Industries, Inc.
201 Flanders Rd.
Westboro (01581)

PPG Industries, Inc.
66 E. Industry Ave.
Springfield (01101)

PPG Industries, Inc.
54 Avon St.
Wakefield (01880)

PPG Industries, Inc.
90 Shrewsbury St.
Worcester (01604)

MICHIGAN

Detroit Metropolitan Area:
Almac Plastics of Michigan, Inc.
P.O. Box 247, South Station
26400 Groesbeck Hwy.
Warren (48090)

Cadillac Plastic & Chemical Co.
Division Dayco Corporation
15111 Second Ave.
Detroit (48203)

MICHIGAN (*cont.*)

Commercial Plastics & Supply
  Corporation
25101 Mound Rd.
Warren (48091)

PPG Industries, Inc.
6045 John C. Lodge Expressway
Detroit (48202)

Cadillac Plastic & Chemical Co.
Division Dayco Corporation
2501 S. Dort Hwy.
Flint (48506)

PPG Industries, Inc.
3230 Robert T. Longway Blvd.
P.O. Box 425
Flint (48506)

Cadillac Plastic & Chemical Co.
Division Dayco Corporation
3015 S. Division
Grand Rapids (49508)

PPG Industries, Inc.
500 Grandville Ave. S.W.
Grand Rapids (49502)

PPG Industries, Inc.
1611 E. Kalamazoo St.
P.O. Box 2177
Lansing (48912)

PPG Industries, Inc.
410 Van Buren St.
Saginaw (48602)

MINNESOTA

Allied Plastics of Duluth, Inc.
831 East Fifth St.
Duluth (55805)

PPG Industries, Inc.
330 Garfield Ave.
P.O. Box 498
Duluth (55801)

Allied Plastics of Minneapolis,
  Inc.
900 Florida Ave. S.
Wayzata Blvd. at Florida
Minneapolis (55426)

Cadillac Plastic & Chemical Co.
Division Dayco Corporation
1607 Hennepin Ave. S.
Minneapolis (55403)

PPG Industries, Inc.
616 S. Third St.
Minneapolis (55414)

Plastics, Inc.
214 Ryan Ave.
St. Paul (55102)

PPG Industries, Inc.
134 E. Ninth St.
St. Paul (55101)

MISSISSIPPI

PPG Industries, Inc.
510 N. Gallatin St.
P.O. Box 1095
Jackson (39203)

MISSOURI

PPG Industries, Inc.
14th St. & Joplin Ave.
Joplin (64803)

Kansas City Metropolitan Area:
Plastic Sales & Manufacturing
  Co., Inc.
3030 McGree Trafficway
Kansas City (64108)

PPG Industries, Inc.
1201 Burlington St.
N. Kansas City (64116)

Regal Plastic Supply Company
2023 Holmes St.
Kansas City (64108)

Transilwrap Company of
  Missouri, Inc.
5720 Brighton St.
Kansas City (64130)

PPG Industries, Inc.
1731 N. Glenstone
P.O. Box 1046, Commercial
  Station
Springfield (65805)

Cadillac Plastic & Chemical Co.
Division Dayco Corporation
8680 Olive St. Rd.
St. Louis (63132)

Cope Plastics Missouri, Inc.
6340 Knox Industrial Dr.
St. Louis (63139)

PPG Industries, Inc.
3650 Market St.
P.O. Box 33
St. Louis (63166)

MONTANA
  Also see WASHINGTON

PPG Industries, Inc.
127 Regal St.
P.O. Box 1197
Billings (59103)

PPG Industries, Inc.
840 Utah Ave.
Butte (59701)

NEBRASKA

PPG Industries, Inc.
318 N. Joseph Ave.
P.O. Box 192
Hastings (68901)

PPG Industries, Inc.
1624 S. 17th St.
Lincoln (68502)

PPG Industries, Inc.
1402 Jones St.
P.O. Box 1049
Omaha (68101)

Regal Plastic Supply Company
2324 Vinton St.
Omaha (68108)

NEW HAMPSHIRE

PPG Industries, Inc.
100 Cahill Ave.
P.O. Box 748
Manchester (03105)

PPG Industries, Inc.
400 Rt. 1 Bypass
Portsmouth (03801)

NEW JERSEY

Newark Metropolitan Area:
Almac Plastics of New Jersey,
  Inc.
171 Fabyan Pl.
Newark (07112)

Cadillac Plastic & Chemical Co.
Division Dayco Corporation
1761 Edgar Rd.
Linden (07036)

Commercial Plastics & Supply
  Corporation
127 Frelinghuysen Ave.
Newark (07108)

PPG Industries, Inc.
99 Murray Hill Pkwy.
E. Rutherford (07073)

Commercial Plastics & Supply
  Corporation
342 Fourth St.
Trenton (08638)

Estok Plastics Company
434 Whitehead Rd.
Trenton (06819)

PPG Industries, Inc.
30 Morse Ave.
Trenton (08638)

NEW MEXICO

PPG Industries, Inc.
601 Haines Ave. N.W.
P.O. Box 741
Albuquerque (87103)

NEW MEXICO (*cont.*)

Regal Plastic Supply Company
3019 Princeton Dr. N.E.
Albuquerque (87107)

NEW YORK

Albany Metropolitan Area:
PPG Industries, Inc.
Wade Rd., P.O. Box 519
Latham (12110)

PPG Industries, Inc.
3 Alice St.
Binghamton (13902)

Cadillac Plastic & Chemical Co.
Division Dayco Corporation
2700 Walden Ave.
Buffalo (14225)

Curbell, Inc.
777 Hertel Ave.
Buffalo (14207)

Great Lakes Plastic Company
2371 Broadway
Buffalo (14212)

PPG Industries, Inc.
803 Walden Ave.
Buffalo (14211)

New York City Metropolitan Area:
Allied Plastics Supply
   Corporation
895 East 167th St.
Bronx (10459)

Almac Plastics, Inc.
47–42 37th St.
Long Island City (11101)

Cadillac Plastic & Chemical Co.
Division Dayco Corporation
35–21 Vernon Blvd.
Long Island City (11106)

Commercial Plastics & Supply
   Corporation
630 Broadway
New York City (10012)

Commercial Plastics & Supply
   Corporation
55 Marine St.
Farmingdale (11735)

Commercial Plastics & Supply
   Corporation
100–02 87th Ave.
Richmond Hill (11418)

Industrial Plastics Supply Co.
309 Canal St.
New York City (10013)

Cadillac Plastic & Chemical Co.
Division Dayco Corporation
295 Buell Rd.
Rochester (14624)

Curbell, Inc.
25 Louise St.
Rochester (14606)

PPG Industries, Inc.
362 Exchange St.
Rochester (14608)

O. D. Blanchard & Bros., Inc.
119 N. Geddes St.
Syracuse (13201)

Curbell, Inc.
100 Danzig St.
Syracuse (13206)

PPG Industries, Inc.
838 Erie Blvd., W.
Syracuse (13204)

PPG Industries, Inc.
210 Factory St.
Watertown (13601)

NORTH CAROLINA

Pritchard Paint & Glass Co.
23 Asheland Ave.
Asheville (28801)

Cadillac Plastic & Chemical Co.
Division Dayco Corporation
3100 South Blvd.
Charlotte (28209)

PPG Industries, Inc.
201 E. Sixth St.
P.O. Box 1396
Charlotte (28201)

Pritchard Paint & Glass Co.
140 Remount Rd.
Charlotte (28203)

Pritchard Paint & Glass Co.
3172 Hillsboro Rd.
Durham (27705)

Engineered Plastics, Inc.
Box 108
Gibsonville (27249)

Engineered Plastics, Inc.
1028 Huffman St.
Greensboro (27405)

PPG Industries, Inc.
109 PPG Rd.
P.O. Box 11404
Greensboro (27409)

Pritchard Paint & Glass Company
161 8th St. Dr., S.E.
Hickory (28601)

Commercial Plastics & Supply
   Corporation
731 W. Hargett St.
Raleigh (27603)

Pritchard Paint & Glass Company
2424 Crabtree Blvd.
Raleigh (27602)

Pritchard Paint & Glass Company
1819 S. Main St.
Salisbury (28144)

OHIO

Almac Plastics of Ohio, Inc.
30 N. Summit St.
Akron (44308)

Cadillac Plastic & Chemical Co.
Division Dayco Corporation
2587 S. Arlington Rd.
Akron (44308)

PPG Industries, Inc.
41 S. Prospect St.
Akron (44308)

Cadillac Plastic & Chemical Co.
Division Dayco Corporation
3818 Red Bank Rd.
Cincinnati (45227)

Cincinnati Plastics
Subsidiary of Dayton Plastics,
   Inc.
90 Terrace Dr.
Cincinnati (45215)

PPG Industries, Inc.
4955 Spring Grove Ave.
Cincinnati (45232)

Cadillac Plastic & Chemical Co.
Division Dayco Corporation
4533 Willow Pkway.
Cleveland (44125)

Transilwrap Company of
   Cleveland
5505 Cloverleaf Pkway.
Cleveland (44125)

Cadillac Plastic & Chemical Co.
Division Dayco Corporation
374 W. Spring St.
Columbus (43215)

PPG Industries, Inc.
2877 Silver Dr.
Columbus (43211)

Dayton Plastics, Inc.
2554 Needmore Rd.
Dayton (45415)

PPG Industries, Inc.
2054 Drill Ave.
Dayton (45414)

OHIO (*cont.*)

PPG Industries, Inc.
750 Bellefontaine Ave.
P.O. Box 126
Lima (45801)

PPG Industries, Inc.
217 Park Ave., E.
Mansfield (44903)

PPG Industries, Inc.
259 Wittenberg Ave.
Springfield (45502)

Cadillac Plastic & Chemical Co.
Division Dayco Corporation
1502 Monroe St.
Toledo (43624)

PPG Industries, Inc.
2742 Hill Ave.
P.O. Box 3473, Station C
Toledo (43607)

PPG Industries, Inc.
2300 E. Highland Rd.
Twinsburg (44807)

PPG Industries, Inc.
25 N. Watt St.
Youngstown (44501)

OKLAHOMA

Cope Plastics Oklahoma, Inc.
105 N.E. 38th Terr.
P.O. Box 53586
Oklahoma City (73105)

PPG Industries, Inc.
4301 N. Santa Fe Blvd.
P.O. Box 9576
Oklahoma City (73108)

Cadillac Plastic & Chemical Co.
Division Dayco Corporation
4920 E. Admiral Pl.
Tulsa (74115)

Plastic Engineering Co. of Tulsa
6801 E. 44th Pl.
P.O. Box 45532
Tulsa (74145)

PPG Industries, Inc.
301 E. Archer St.
P.O. Box 1120
Tulsa (74101)

OREGON

Universal Plastics Company
910 S.E. Stark St.
Portland (97214)

PENNSYLVANIA

Plastic Mart
340 N. Ninth St.
Allentown (18102)

PPG Industries, Inc.
1627 Sumner Ave.
Allentown (18105)

PPG Industries, Inc.
3600 Beale Ave.
P.O. Box 671
Altoona (16603)

PPG Industries, Inc.
19 W. Second St.
P.O. Box 736
Erie (16512)

PPG Industries, Inc.
881 Eisenhower Blvd.
P.O. Box 2055
Harrisburg (17105)

PPG Industries, Inc.
252 N. Prince St.
P.O. Box 178
Lancaster (17604)

PPG Industries, Inc.
Route 8
P.O. Box 610
Oil City (16301)

Philadelphia Metropolitan Area:
Almac Plastics of Pennsylvania,
   Inc.
2031 Byberry Rd.
Philadelphia (19116)

Cadillac Plastic & Chemical Co.
Division Dayco Corporation
Airport Industrial Park
Pennsauken, N.J. (08109)

Commercial Plastics & Supply
  Corporation
7332 Milnor St.
Philadelphia (19135)

Crystal-X Corporation
Second & Pine Sts.
Darby (19023)

Plastics of Philadelphia
Corner 12th & Arch Sts.
Philadelphia (19107)

PPG Industries, Inc.
2629 N. 15th St.
Philadelphia (19132)

Transilwrap Company of
  Philadelphia, Inc.
2741 N. Fourth St.
Philadelphia (19133)

Pittsburgh Metropolitan Area:
Cadillac Plastic & Chemical Co.
Division Dayco Corporation
600 Seco Rd.
Monroeville (15146)

Commercial Plastics & Supply
  Corporation
2022 Chateau St.
Pittsburgh (15233)

PPG Industries, Inc.
632 Ft. Duquesne Blvd.
Pittsburgh (15222)

PPG Industries, Inc.
823 Wyoming Ave.
Scranton (18509)

RHODE ISLAND

Commercial Plastics & Supply
  Corporation
920 Broadway
E. Providence (02914)

PPG Industries, Inc.
350 Kinsley Ave.
Providence (02901)

SOUTH CAROLINA

PPG Industries, Inc.
804 Meeting St.
P.O. Box 6128
Charleston (29403)

PPG Industries, Inc.
1615 Barnwell St., Myers Branch
P.O. Box 1767
Columbia (29202)

Engineered Plastics, Inc.
Industrial Dr.
Pleasantburg Industrial Park
Greenville (29607)

PPG Industries, Inc.
401 Rhett St.
P.O. Box 2285
Greenville (29602)

Pritchard Paint & Glass Co.
1185 E. Main St.
Rock Hill (29730)

PPG Industries, Inc.
197 E. St. John St.
P.O. Box 326
Spartanburg (29301)

SOUTH DAKOTA
  Also see MINNESOTA

PPG Industries, Inc.
434 N. Main Ave.
P.O. Box 1144
Sioux Falls (57101)

TENNESSEE

PPG Industries, Inc.
439 Airways Blvd.
P.O. Box 1625
Jackson (38301)

TENNESSEE (*cont.*)

PPG Industries, Inc.
207 Humes St.
Knoxville (37917)

Norrell, Inc.
3496 Winhoma Dr.
P.O. Box 30279
Memphis (38130)

PPG Industries, Inc.
435 Madison Ave.
Memphis (38103)

Plastic Supply & Mfg. Company
1319 Lewis St.
Nashville (37210)

PPG Industries, Inc.
1102 Grundy St.
Nashville (37203)

TEXAS

PPG Industries, Inc.
801 Grant St.
P.O. Box 630
Amarillo (79105)

PPG Industries, Inc.
205 W. Fifth St.
P.O. Box 1606
Austin (78701)

PPG Industries, Inc.
901 Pearl St.
Beaumont (77701)

PPG Industries, Inc.
402 N. Port Ave.
P.O. Box 4769
Corpus Christi (78408)

A-1 Plastics Supply Company
13700 Gamma Rd.
Dallas (75240)

Cadillac Plastic & Chemical Co.
Division Dayco Corporation
2546 Irving Blvd.
Dallas (75207)

Commercial Plastics & Supply
Corporation
Wycliff & Vantage Sts.
Dallas (75207)

PPG Industries, Inc.
1421 N. Industrial Blvd.
P.O. Box 10327
Dallas (75207)

Baker Glass and Plastics
4015 Montana Ave.
P.O. Box 3896
El Paso (79903)

PPG Industries, Inc.
1106 E. Overland St.
P.O. Box 1708
El Paso (79949)

Cadillac Plastic & Chemical Co.
Division Dayco Corporation
1400 Henderson St.
Ft. Worth (76102)

PPG Industries, Inc.
1825 Main St.
P.O. Box 1928
Ft. Worth (76101)

PPG Industries, Inc.
628 Tremont St.
Galveston (77550)

C. P. Waggoner Sales Company,
Inc.
233 S.E. 14th St.
Grand Prairie (75050)

PPG Industries, Inc.
1110 W. Jackson St.
P.O. Box 1806
Harlingen (78551)

A-1 Plastics of Houston, Inc.
5822 Southwest Freeway
Houston (77027)

Cadillac Plastic & Chemical Co.
Division Dayco Corporation
5031 Gulf Freeway
Houston (77023)

Commercial Plastics
7406 Lawndale Ave.
Houston (77035)

Plasteco, Inc.
P.O. Box 9485
8535 Market St. Rd.
Houston (77011)

PPG Industries, Inc.
5520 Armour Dr.
P.O. Box 1433
Houston (77001)

PPG Industries, Inc.
611 23rd St.
P.O. Box 248
Lubbock (79408)

PPG Industries, Inc.
1420 S. Alamo St.
P.O. Box 459
San Antonio (78206)

Reece Supply Co. of San Antonio
714 W. Craig St.
San Antonio (78212)

PPG Industries, Inc.
305 E. Goodwin Ave.
P.O. Box 2116
Victoria (77901)

UTAH

Bennett's
65 W. First, S.
Salt Lake City (84110)

Plastics Products Co. of Utah
2340 S. Temple, W.
Salt Lake City (84110)

VERMONT
    Also see CONNECTICUT
PPG Industries, Inc.
358 Dorset St.
Burlington (05401)

VIRGINIA
PPG Industries, Inc.
503 Loyal St.
P.O. Box 881
Danville (24541)

PPG Industries, Inc.
2201 Colonial Ave.
Norfolk (23517)

Read Plastic Materials
    Corporation
2442 Ingleside Dr.
Norfolk (23513)

Engineered Plastics Inc.
5410 Distributor Dr.
Richmond (23224)

Plywood and Plastics, Inc.
P.O. Box 6592
1727 Arlington Rd.
Richmond (23230)

PPG Industries, Inc.
2210 Magnolia St.
Richmond (23223)

PPG Industries, Inc.
1814 Jefferson St., S.E.
P.O. Box 8396
Roanoke (24014)

WASHINGTON

Cadillac Plastic & Chemical Co.
Division Dayco Corporation
2427 Sixth Ave., S.
Seattle (98134)

Universal Plastics Company
650 S. Adams St.
Seattle (98108)

WEST VIRGINIA
    Also see PENNSYLVANIA

PPG Industries, Inc.
600 Virginia St., W.
Charleston (25302)

WISCONSIN

PPG Industries, Inc.
2042 Gross Ave.
P.O. Box 3264
Green Bay (54303)

WISCONSIN (*cont.*)

PPG Industries, Inc.
59 Copeland Ave.
P.O. Box 704
Lacrosse (54601)

Milwaukee Metropolitan Area:
Cadillac Plastic & Chemical Co.
Division Dayco Corporation
4821 N. 32nd
Milwaukee (53209)

Colonial Kolonite Corporation of
    Wisconsin
12300 W. Adler La.
West Allis (53214)

Midland Plastics, Inc.
3605 N. 126th St.
Brookfield (53005)

PPG Industries, Inc.
11316 W. Rogers St.
P.O. Box 724
Milwaukee (53201)

PPG Industries, Inc.
208 Division St.
P.O. Box 128
Oshkosh (54902)

PPG Industries, Inc.
2617 Lathrop Ave.
P.O. Box 1307
Racine (53405)

PPG Industries, Inc.
729 Forest St.
P.O. Box 989
Wausau (54401)

Accessory Suppliers

CEMENT

Guard Coatings and Chemicals
58 John Hay Ave.
Kearny, N.J. (07032)

Schwartz Chemical Company,
   Inc.
50–01 Second St.
Long Island City, N.Y. (11101)

STRIP HEATERS

Hydor Therme Corporation
7155 Airport Hwy.
Pennsauken, N.J. (08109)

For approved accessory products for working with acrylic sheet, including cutting tools, solvent, cement, solvent applicator, thickened cements, strip heater elements, buffing kits, and cleaner/polish, write to:

Tools for Plexiglas
P.O. Box 14619
Philadelphia, Pa. (19134)